PHIZ

Illustrations from the Novels of

CHARLES DICKENS

PHIZ

Illustrations from the Novels of

CHARLES DICKENS

By

Albert Johannsen [Pseud] (Browne, Hablot Knight)

THE UNIVERSITY OF CHICAGO PRESS

47679

Library of Congress Catalog Number: 56-10998

THE UNIVERSITY OF CHICAGO PRESS, CHICAGO 37
Cambridge University Press, London, N.W. 1, England
The University of Toronto Press, Toronto 5, Canada

© 1956 by The University of Chicago. Published 1956
Composed and printed by THE UNIVERSITY OF CHICAGO
PRESS, *Chicago, Illinois, U.S.A.*

Preface

The plates used in illustrating the novels of Dickens, Ainsworth, Lever, and others, though generally spoken of as steel engravings, are actually etchings. A steel engraving is printed from a plate upon which the design is incised with a graver. An etching, on the other hand, begins with a design drawn in reverse upon a wax-coated plate. Subsequently the lines are traced with a sharp-pointed instrument to cut through the wax and expose the metal; then the plate is immersed in acid until the picture is bitten in.

It is unnecessary to give here more than a brief outline of the story of the etching of the "Phiz" plates. The first etchings by Seymour for *Pickwick* were on poor steel and needed such frequent retouching that they finally broke down completely and new plates had to be made. Later, with better material, most of the plates for seven of Dickens' major works were etched in duplicate, triplicate, or even in quadruplicate, in order to keep pace with the more rapid printing of the letterpress. The number of steels, therefore, for these seven novels was greater than the number of plates which appeared in the published books. A few plates for *Pickwick* were etched on steels the size of a single print, but later all the steels were twice the size of the plates, and two designs were etched on each. At first, different illustrations were drawn on the two halves, but afterward the original etching and its duplicate were made on the same plate. After printing, the etchings were cut apart, sent to the binder, and indiscriminately inserted in the monthly parts of the novels.

This, briefly, accounts for the mixture of plates in different copies of the books, but *all of them are first editions for they were issued simultaneously*. In some cases it is possible to determine which of the steels were etched first, but in the majority this is not possible.

Of all the plates for Dickens' novels, the first four from *Pickwick* have been most thoroughly studied. They have been described in words by Thomson, Kitton, Hatton and Cleaver, Miller and Strange, Bay, and others, but the remaining plates have been almost totally neglected or dismissed with the statement that "the differences are slight and are shown principally in variations in the artist's signature." Actually, there is considerable difference in some plates, while in a few close examination is necessary to determine whether they are new or only old ones that have been retouched.

For the seven novels showing duplication, "Phiz" etched 490 different steels (or 496 if Pls. 40 and 41 of *Pickwick* and 3–6 of *Nickleby* were in fact etched in triplicate). For *Pickwick* he etched 77 (or 79); for *Nickleby* 125 (or 129); for *Chuzzlewit* 90; for *Dombey and Son* 80; for *David Copperfield* 80; for *Bleak House* 20; and for *Little Dorrit* 18. This enumeration of duplicated plates naturally does not include the plates etched only once for *Bleak House* and *Little Dorrit*, the plates in *A Tale of Two Cities*, the retouched plates, the woodcuts in *Barnaby Rudge* and *The Old Curiosity Shop*, or the plates etched by other artists for *Sketches by Boz*, *Oliver Twist*, *Our Mutual Friend*, and

Edwin Drood. There are a number of retouched plates which are not reproduced in this book, but the 19 new designs from the 1838 edition of *Pickwick* are.

There seems to be a general but mistaken belief that George Cruikshank was the chief illustrator of the novels of Dickens, and even booksellers occasionally refer to the original etchings in these novels as "by Cruikshank." Perhaps this idea started because Cruikshank illustrated a couple of Dickens' early books or perhaps because Cruikshank was an established etcher before Hablôt Knight Browne ("Phiz") began his career as an artist. How incorrect this is may be seen by a comparison of the number of illustrations made for these novels by different artists.

Listing the plates in *all* of Dickens' novels, we find that George Cruikshank made 40 plates for *Sketches by Boz* and 24 for *Oliver Twist*. Robert Seymour made 7 for *Pickwick*, and Robert Buss made 2 for the same book. Hablôt K. Browne, however, made a total of 567 (or 573) steels for *Pickwick, Martin Chuzzlewit, Nicholas Nickleby, Dombey and Son, David Copperfield, Bleak House, Little Dorrit*, and *A Tale of Two Cities*. In addition, he made the drawings for six woodcuts for *Sunday under Three Heads*, seven for the wrappers of the monthly parts, 157 for *Master Humphrey's Clock* (which includes *Old Curiosity Shop* and *Barnaby Rudge*) and 866 for the "Household" edition. Finally, there were also 39 woodcuts by George Cattermole for *Master Humphrey's Clock*, one by S. Williams and one by Samuel Maclise for the same book, 40 woodcuts by Marcus Stone for *Our Mutual Friend*, and 14 woodcuts by Luke Fildes for *The Mystery of Edwin Drood*. By Cruikshank, therefore, there was a total of 64 illustrations as against 1,603 by "Phiz," or, omitting the woodcuts for the "Household" edition, as against a total of 737. This summary should disprove the claim that George Cruikshank was the most important of Dickens' artists.

It may come as a surprise to some Dickens lovers to learn of the lengths to which a rabid Dickensian will go to complete his collection. To obtain from the seven major Dickens novels all the 516 plates given in this book, it was necessary to break up twelve first editions of *Pickwick* (plus a much rarer bound volume of the 1838 edition), fifteen of *Nickleby*, nine of *Chuzzlewit*, nine of *Copperfield*, seven of *Dombey*, six of *Bleak House*, and eight of *Little Dorrit*, a total of sixty-six copies. This may seem vandalism to those whose prized possession is a single *Pickwick*. Naturally, while those broken up were all first editions, only a few were in the wrappers as issued. Most of them were copies which had been bound from the parts before wrappers and advertisements were regarded more highly than the text itself! However, for the purpose of this book, copies in the parts were not absolutely necessary, provided that the plates in the bound first editions were clear impressions. While a prime *Pickwick* in the parts as issued has a record sale price of twenty-six thousand dollars, a moderately satisfactory copy in parts may be obtained for three hundred dollars or less, while *Bleak House, Little Dorrit*, and *Edwin Drood* may be picked up for much less than fifty dollars. Personally I have never paid an exorbitant price for any Dickens novel, but many of my copies were bought forty or fifty years ago, and prices have greatly increased since then, or our dollars have greatly decreased in value, or both.

The search for a set of all the plates has been a long one. My first *Pickwick* was bought in 1903, and, as I could not examine all copies put up for sale at book auctions, I was obliged at first to buy copies as offered, sight unseen, in the hopes that some of the plates missing in my collection would be present. When most of these had been obtained by random buying, I made enlarged photographs of those whose duplicates I lacked, and, with these available, it was a simple matter in bookstores to "spot" missing plates. For the final few plates, I sent the photographs to dealers in this country and in London, and this eventually brought the remainder of the set as here given.

A reproduction of a print from each of the different steels is given in this book and also in a few cases examples of retouched plates. The existence of third steels, mentioned by Croal Thomson and by Hatton and Cleaver, for the plates in Parts II and III of *Nicholas Nickleby* seems to me to be somewhat questionable. Even a search by me in London and later by several London booksellers failed to unearth any plates showing greater variations from the originals than do those shown as "B₂" of Plates 3, 4, 5, and 6 of *Nickleby*. If these four "B₂" plates are from new steels, they were so slavishly copied that the resemblance to the "B₁" plates is extremely close, even to the number of shade lines in the drawing. Background and foreground foliage differ in places, but that may represent only a re-engraving of much-worn parts. Even differences in lengths of the legends beneath the etchings, as seen, for example, in "B₁" and "B₂" of Plate 4 of *Nickleby*, may represent worn lines burnished out and recut.

On the following pages I have listed some of the more easily recognizable variations in the plates. While some plates bear numbers which differentiate them, these may be hard to find, owing to worn steels or careless printing. Plates which have been cleaned also may have lost their numbers, their signatures, or other details, especially around the edges. There are, of course, many other differences than those listed in the descriptions which follow, some of them easy to see but hard to describe in words.

Many of Browne's original steels remained in the hands of the publishers, Chapman and Hall, these many years, until about twenty-five years ago some of the duplicate plates were sold to a London bookseller. In 1937, just one hundred years after the publication of *Pickwick*, the remaining 877 steels and woodcuts were used in printing the twenty-three volumes of the "Nonesuch Dickens," and after publication each subscriber received one of the original plates. I am fortunate in having in my possession the steel plates of 6-C, 24-B, 30-B, 31-B, and 34-B of *Martin Chuzzlewit* and 15-A, 20-A, 26-B, and 31-B of *Dombey and Son*. I also have the original wood block by Marcus Stone of "Lady Jane Grey" from *The Child's History of England*.

Some attempt was made to discover a significance in the various curlicues and dots in the artist's signatures as indicating the sequence of the engraving, but after some apparent order seemed to have been found, a new signature would discredit it. Perhaps it may amuse some readers when tired of crossword puzzles to try to find a secret code to the sequence of the plates, which many Dickensians think exists.

ALBERT JOHANNSEN

References

BAY, J. CHRISTIAN. "The Pickwick Papers," *Amateur Book Collector*, I, No. 4 (December, 1950), 7–8.

BROWNE, EDGAR. *Phiz and Dickens*. London, 1913.

DEXTER, JOHN F. *Hints to Dickens Collectors*. London, 1884.

DEXTER, WALTER, and LEY, J. W. T. *The Origin of Pickwick*. London, 1936.

ECKEL, JOHN C. *The First Editions of the Writings of Charles Dickens, Their Points and Values: A Bibliography*. New York and London, 1932.

HATTON, THOMAS, and CLEAVER, ARTHUR H. *A Bibliography of the Periodical Works of Charles Dickens: Bibliographical, Analytical, and Statistical*. London, 1933.

JOHNSON, CHARLES PLUMPTRE. *Hints to Collectors of the Original Editions of the Works of Charles Dickens*. London, 1885.

KITTON, FREDERIC G. *Dickens and His Illustrators*. London, 1899.

———. *A Bibliography of the Literature Relating to Charles Dickens and His Writings*. London, 1886.

———. *Charles Dickens by Pen and Pencil*. London, 1890.

MILLER, W., and STRANGE, E. H. "The Original Pickwick Papers: The Collation of a Perfect First Edition," *Dickensian*, XXIX (1933), 303–9; XXX (1934), 31–37, 121–24, 177–80, 249–59.

THOMSON, DAVID CROAL. *Life and Labours of Hablôt Knight Browne, "Phiz."* London, 1884.

Hablôt Knight Browne

Hablôt Knight Browne, the artist, was born in 1815. Even as a boy, his talent for drawing was recognized, and as a consequence he was apprenticed to the engraver Finden. Browne wanted to be a painter, and the tedious work of engraving irked him. He was of an imaginative turn of mind, and he found more pleasure in drawing caricatures than in attending to his work with the graver. Finden and he were mutually unhappy over this situation so that both were well satisfied when he finally obtained release from his indentures, and in 1834, at the age of nineteen, he set himself up as an independent artist. Before leaving Finden, however, he had had some part in twenty-six of the drawings for the first volume of Henry Winkles' proposed book on the *Cathedrals of England*.

Between 1834 and 1836 Browne seems to have done only occasional work here and there, but after Seymour, the artist of the first seven etchings for *Pickwick*, died in 1836 and was followed by Buss with two crude and unsatisfastory etchings, he submitted specimens of his work to Dickens, who thought them very satisfactory. Browne was already known to Dickens, for he had earlier in the same year made six sketches for "Sunday under Three Heads." The collaboration of Browne and Dickens thus begun continued uninterruptedly for twenty-three years until the conclusion of *A Tale of Two Cities* in December, 1859; during that time he made some 724 drawings for him, of which 567 were etched and 157 engraved on wood. During the two years of the *Pickwick* production, he had hardly begun to be known, and relatively few other etchings were made. Later, and concurrently with the Dickens plates, he was also etching plates for Lever, Ainsworth, Smedley, and other writers, so that between the beginning of *Pickwick* and the ending of *A Tale of Two Cities*, he made over 2,200 etchings and woodcuts. Never working on Sundays, he averaged about eight drawings a month. He himself figured, at the time he was working on the Dickens books, that he was etching four steels in ten working days, a remarkable record, considering that he made the drawings, submitted them for correction, redrew and transferred them to the steels, and cut the lines in the wax and at first did much of the biting in also.

After his last work for Dickens, his production fell off somewhat, so that in the years following, until his right arm became partially paralyzed by a stroke in 1867, he produced only 440 drawings, and afterward about 1,000 more. Of these, 866 were for the woodcuts used in 1874 in the "Household" edition of Dickens, all of them rather poor and falling far short of his previous work. However, in these and later years, after the demand for steel etchings had dwindled, he continued with some success to produce water colors.

On July 8, 1882, Browne died at the age of sixty-seven, a great artist to whom Dickens is indebted for much of the popularity of his books.

The *Posthumous Papers* *of*

THE PICKWICK CLUB

In April, 1836, Chapman and Hall issued in London the first number of a humorous publication which, after the lapse of over one hundred years, is just as readable as when it first appeared. As were most of Dickens' major works, *The Pickwick Papers*, as they are generally called, appeared in twenty parts, the first eighteen at monthly intervals, the nineteenth and twentieth together in November, 1837, as the final number. Originally it was intended that each shilling number should consist of 24 pages of text and four etchings, and thus Part I appeared. Owing to the death of the artist, Robert Seymour, before the four etchings for Part II were completed, this number contained only three. The plan was then altered to keep the cost of production down, and, beginning with Part III and continuing to the end, there were 32 pages of text and two etchings in each part.

At first, on account of the wearing-down of the steel plates upon which the designs were etched and later to the need for quicker printing of the plates to keep pace with the printing of the text, duplicate steels were made, in most cases following the originals very closely but in some cases departing radically from them. Apparently, a proof was pulled from the first plate and transferred to the wax of the second, and then traced either by Browne himself or by his assistant Robert Young, or later by some other assistant. Besides this duplication of plates, there was another cause for slight variations in the prints, for, as the plates wore down, they were repeatedly touched up and strengthened by crosshatching or recutting. These minor variations are, in general, insignificant and are not mentioned in the following pages unless the changes were fairly great.

The original plates for Parts I and II (Pls. 1–7) were by Robert Seymour, and those in Part III (Pls. 8 and 9) by Robert Buss, but they are given here for comparison with the later plates by Browne. Altogether, there were 45 different designs in *Pickwick*: 43 original plates plus 2 by Browne as substitutes for the unsatisfactory Buss plates (Pls. 8 and 9). To these should be added as varieties 4 duplicate plates (1–4) etched by Seymour; 4 Seymour plates copied by Browne (1–4); 15 plates by Browne for the edition of 1838, with engraved titles to replace Plates 5–7 and 10–21, inclusive; 18 by Browne as duplicates of Plates

22–39, inclusive; 2 (or 4) plates by Browne representing duplicates (or triplicates) of Plates 40 and 41; and 2 plates by Browne as duplicates of the Frontispiece and the etched title, making a total of 90 (or 92) plates necessary to include all major varieties. The two extra Plates 40 and 41, just mentioned, which appear to me to be simply retouched steels and not new ones, are fully described later. The total varieties may be increased by including various plate states, the transposed page numbers on Plates 14 and 15, the unnumbered Plates 26 and 27, and the second "Phiz" plates (22–41) with the added legends as given in the 1838 bound volume. These, however, are not new plates and, of course, show no changes in the designs themselves. They are, therefore, not included in the count.

The steel plates for *Pickwick*, with one exception, were all double the size of the etchings, and each had two designs. They were printed simultaneously and afterward cut apart. "The Dying Clown," No. 5, was the exception, being alone on an octavo steel. Since duplication was not decided on until later, the first nine parts, including Plates 1–21, had two different subjects on each steel, but from Plate 22 to the end, the duplicates were side by side on the same steel.

Properly, of course, Plates 1–9 of the first printings do not belong among the "Phiz" etchings except as showing the originals which he copied. And as for the first copies of the first four Seymour plates, even the great authorities do not agree on the artist. John F. Dexter (originally in 1884), David Croal Thomson (1884), and Frederic G. Kitton (1889) regarded the first duplicates as copies by "Phiz" of the Seymour designs. Later Dexter, in a letter written in September, 1909, said that he and F. W. Pailthorpe, an artist and etcher, had spent considerable time three or four years previously over these etchings. They came to the conclusion that "there is not a trace of Phiz's work in them. Seymour in his private diary states that he etched a second set of plates without giving any reason for it, so I suggested to Mr. Pailthorpe that probably Seymour took an impression in red ink from the first set of plates, transferred this impression on to a new waxed steel plate and that this would account for the slavishness of the copy. . . . Mr. Pailthorp accepted this suggestion at once and I think that it is undoubtedly a correct solution of the question."

Hatton and Cleaver (1933) accepted Dexter's conclusion that the third etchings of Plates 1–4 which appeared with engraved legends in the bound volume in 1838 were the first copies made by "Phiz." I entirely agree with this, and in confirmation, as I point out later where the individual plates are described, is the fact that Seymour in his signature "Seymour, del" used an ordinary Latin cursive letter *d*, while "Phiz" in the later copy, which also had Seymour's name, used his usual Greek δ.

Because the original Seymour steels were retouched and patched until they collapsed, the printed plates show considerable variation. Said John F. Dexter:[1] "In the first issue of 400 copies of Part I, the [first] plates are mostly brilliant impressions, but tailing off sadly when you come towards the 400th copy, so much so, that I have seen absolute skeletons of the plates which I presume to be within the 3rd and 4th hundred. . . . I have never seen more than twelve copies in parts right all the way through during the whole time that I have been collecting and perhaps some of these twelve I may have seen for the second time where they have occurred for sale." Furthermore, according to Hatton and Cleaver,[2] Dexter wrote, on the margin of one of his bibliographies: "I very much doubt whether more than 50 impressions in first state were obtained from the first set of steels."

1. Letter of September, 1909, now in my possession.

2. (2d ed., 1933), p. 19.

Part I · Plate 1 · Page 2

Mr. Pickwick Addresses the Club

[PLATE A]

Original Plate by Seymour

As just mentioned, there are numerous states of Plate 1, as shown by slight, progressive changes in shading, strengthening of lines, and so on, but too unimportant to chronicle. However, the main characteristics of the original plate remain the same throughout. They serve to separate it from the duplicate plate which was etched by Seymour to take the place of the original after some 400 impressions had been taken from it. While artistically this plate leaves much to be desired, it must be conceded that Mr. Pickwick's portrait follows the text so closely (or vice versa) that in all the numerous drawings that have been made of him by other artists in later years, only those that follow the original pattern satisfy. Disregarding slight changes made in retouching, the original plate shows:

a) The buttons of Mr. Pickwick's vest are properly placed at the right of the parting line, that is, toward his left side.

b) There are only two books in front of the Secretary, although at first sight there appear to be three.

c) The shading of the floor boards and of the space between the dog and the Secretary's leg was done freehand and was not ruled.

d) The picture of Pickwick back of the chandelier has a double cord at the right, and at the left side and bottom of the frame are scallops to represent shadows.

e) The signature, *Seymour, del*, in script occurs at the lower left and is quite readable in early impressions. The letter *d* of *del* is in ordinary Latin cursive.

f) The meeting line of Tupman's vest in early impressions shows as a faint white line; later it shows as a strong black line.

page: 2

g) The *g* of the page number beneath the design shows a curly tail.

h) The left ends of the fishing rods are tied in a round bundle with two separate cords.

i) The rear leg of the chair near the left margin is very near the line of junction between two floor boards.

k) The stem of the churchwarden in the hand of the man at the head of the table is shown by a double line.

l) The pupils of Mr. Tupman's eyes are turned so far upward that they hardly show, and those of the third man on the left are turned to his right.

page 2

[P L A T E B]

Duplicate Etched by Seymour

Mr Pickwick addresses the club.

After the first steel had been in use only a month, it was copied on a second plate in April, 1836. As mentioned previously, this is *not* a copy by Browne but by Seymour himself. In general, it follows the original very closely but differs in many minor points:

a) The buttons on Mr. Pickwick's vest are now incorrectly placed on the left of the parting, that is, toward Mr. Pickwick's right side.
b) There are three books in front of the Secretary.
c) The floor is shaded by ruled lines.

d) The picture back of the chandelier has a single cord at the right, and there is no scalloped shading at the side and bottom.
e) The signature is plainer than in the first plate, but, like it, the letters are in script and the *d* of *del* is the Latin form.
f) Tupman's vest meets in a black line, as in the later impressions of the first plate, and there are numerous lines crossing it.
g) The *g* of the page number does not have a little curl at the end.

h) The left ends of the fishing rods do not show as separate poles but as a flattened oval of overlapping loops. The left end is now tied with a single cord, which passes around the rods several times and close together.

i) The rear leg of the chair near the left margin is not so close to a floor crack.

k) The stem of the churchwarden in the hand of the man at the head of the table is shown by a single line.

l) The pupils of Mr. Tupman's eyes show clearly. Those of the third man from the left are as in Plate A.

[PLATE C]

Duplicate Plate Etched by Browne for the Edition of 1838

The third steel was etched by Browne but signed with Seymour's name, since it was a copy of the earlier plate. It was used only in the bound volume of 1838 and never in the separate parts. It has an engraved (not etched) legend instead of a page number, and below that, as in all the plates in the bound volume, are the publishers' name and address.

The bound volume with engraved titles is probably rarer than the earlier editions. The following points separate Plate C from the preceding two.

a) The buttons on Mr. Pickwick's vest are incorrectly placed, as in Plate B.

b) There are three books in front of the Secretary, as in Plate B.

c) The floor boards are again etched freehand, as in Plate A.

d) The picture back of the chandelier has no cord at all. The shading at the left and below is by a second straight line.

e) The signature, *Seymour, del.*, is very clear, but it is not in Seymour's style, and the *d* of *del.* is the typical Greek δ, looking like a figure 8, as used by "Phiz."

f) Tupman's vest is dark, but there is neither a white nor a sharp black line, as in Plates A and B.

g) Instead of a page number, the plate has the legend *Mr. Pickwick addresses the Club.*

h) The left ends of the fishing rods show as separate poles, but, unlike Plate A, they are not in a round bundle but are spread out. There is no cord tying them at the left.

i) The leg of the chair as in Plate B.

k) The stem of Joseph Smiggers' pipe is a single line, as in Plate B.

l) Tupman's eyes are not so large and show no lower lids. Those of the third man from the left with the burnsides are looking downward.

Part I · Plate 2 · Page 7

The Pugnacious Cabman

Like the preceding, this plate was repeatedly worked over until it was worn out, and a new plate was etched by Seymour in April, 1836, after the original had been in use only a month. A third plate was made by Browne in 1838 for the bound volume, but the Seymour signature was retained.

page 7

[PLATE A]

Original Plate by Seymour

a) The end of the carpetbag lying at Mr. Pickwick's feet shows diagonal lines which are nearly straight.

b) The tall soldier in the background at the right has no mustache.

c) The milkmaid at the left is clearly shown in early impressions, but she becomes fainter in later printings.

d) The signature *Seymour* is quite legible in early impressions but fades out in the later ones.

e) The right shoulder of the man between the horse's head and Pickwick's shoulder is shaded.

f) The man who appears over the pugnacious cabman's right shoulder wears a stovepipe hat.

g) Pickwick's coat collar in first impressions is bounded below by a white line, but in retouched copies this have been obliterated by widening the collar.

h) The glasses on the ground near Mr. Pickwick's feet have one temple turned in.

i) The *g* of the word *page* below the design has a curly tail.

k) Most of the pieman's left foot is on the walk.

[PLATE B]

Duplicate Etched by Seymour

a) The end of the carpetbag shows one double and one single curved line.

b) The tall soldier has a mustache, and the background about his head is less hazy than before.

c) The milkmaid is faintly etched.

d) The signature is very faint.

e) The right shoulder of the man whose head shows between the horse's mouth and Pickwick's shoulder is white.

f) The man whose head appears over the pugnacious cabman's right shoulder wears a round-crowned hat.

g) Pickwick's collar is as in the later impressions of Plate A.

h) The glasses on the ground are as in Plate A.

i) The *g* of the word *page* ends in a smooth curve.

k) Most of the pieman's left foot is on the walk.

page - 7.

The pugnacious cabman.

[P L A T E C]

Copy of Seymour's Plate Etched by "Phiz" for the Bound Volume of 1838

a) There are three curved diagonal lines on the end of the carpetbag.
b) As in Plate B.
c) The milkmaid is bolder.
d) The signature is strong, with the name *Seymour* spelled with a Greek ϵ, a misshapen *y*, script letters *n* and *o*, and capital letters *U* and *R*.

e) As in Plate A.
f) The man's hat has a somewhat damaged round crown.
g) As in Plate B.
h) The glasses have the temple turned outward.
i) In the place of the page number there is now the legend *The pugnacious cabman.*
k) The pieman's left foot is entirely on the cobblestones.

Part I · Plate 3 · Page 9

The Sagacious Dog

The third plate of *The Pickwick Papers*, like the first two and the fourth, was etched twice by Seymour and later a third time by Browne for the edition of 1838. The first plate was retouched several times, and there is some difference of opinion as to which is the first state. However, there is agreement as to the steels themselves.

[P L A T E A]

Original Plate Etched by Seymour

a) The gun on Jingle's shoulder (not the gamekeeper's, as Hatton and Cleaver say) must have both hammer and trigger. In early impressions, according to Hatton and Cleaver, there is a small break between the gun barrel and Jingle's hair, showing as a thin white line. J. Christian Bay,[3] however, says: "The white line should be excluded without delay from our diagnosis," and adds that it is shown halfway across the barrel in the first state, not at all in what he calls the second, and all the way across in what he calls the third. (I disagree with Dr. Bay in his assignment of second place to the plate with the hammer showing a two-point connection with the gun. This is the plate in this book called Plate C and occurs with inscriptions beneath the design.) The white line occurs in some copies but is cut off below by a thin black line which lies below the gun barrel.

3. J. Christian Bay, "The Pickwick Papers," *Amateur Book Collector*, I (December, 1950), 7–8.

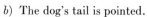

page. 9.

Second Plate Etched by Seymour

b) The dog's tail is pointed.

c) The hinges of the gate are shaded by vertical lines.

d) The hasp on the gatepost stands out sharply from the foliage.

e) The signature *Seymour, del* in the lower center may be faint but distinct, or almost invisible, depending upon the impression. The *d* of *del* is of the usual Latin type.

f) The shading on Jingle's coat cuff is around the arm.

g) In the page number below the design, the letter *p* begins with a single downstroke. The *g* shows a curve upward in the tail but not a return to the right. There is no legend.

a) The gun on Jingle's shoulder has no hammer (Hatton and Cleaver, by mistake, say "no trigger"), but it has a trigger and trigger guard. In early impressions there is a white line extending entirely across the gun barrel, *not* between the gun and Jingle's hair, but between a single hair line and the rest of his hair. In worked-over plates this white line is filled in.

b) The dog's tail is rounded at the end, which is entirely white.

c) The hinges of the gate are unshaded.

d) The hasp on the gatepost does not stand out so sharply from the foliage, especially in the later impressions.

The sagacious dog.

e) The signature is very clear and dark.
f) The shading of Jingle's coat cuff is parallel to the length of his arm.
g) The letter *p* of the page number begins with an upstroke, so that the stem is double. The *g* shows a distinct hook. There is no legend.

This plate, as well as the first Seymour, was retouched, and in the later impressions there are many slight changes. For example, the side rails of the steps show many horizontal lines across the top, and the boards of the fence show that many of the lines have been strengthened.

Copy of Seymour's Plate Etched by Browne for the 1838 Edition

a) The gun on Jingle's shoulder has a larger hammer, which has two points of contact with the barrel. Jingle's hair has obliterated the white line separating it from the gun barrel.
b) The dog's tail is much like that of the original plate.
c) The hinges of the gate are shaded, as in Plate A.
d) There is no hasp on the gatepost.
e) The signature *Seymour, del* is entirely different from Seymour's own. "Phiz" in his copy used a Greek ε and ended with a capital *R*. The *d* of *del* looks like a Greek δ.
f) Jingle's coat cuff is very dark. The shading consists of lines around the arm and diagonals.
g) There is no page number, but, instead, the legend *The sagacious dog* has been added.

Although the copy is very faithful, there are many variations in the rendering. The foliage is different in both the background and the foreground, there are extra horizontal shade lines beneath the steps, and so on.

Part I · Plate 4 · Page 17

Dr. Slammer's Defiance of Jingle

This plate, the fourth in Part I and the last one that was etched twice by Seymour, was, like the preceding ones, later copied by Browne. The differences are not great but distinct enough to make the separation easy.

[P L A T E A]

Original Plate Etched by Seymour

a) There are ten floor boards.
b) Dr. Slammer's left foot does not touch the crack in the floor, and Jingle's left foot is in the center of the second board, while his right foot is entirely on the narrow second step.

page - 17

page - 17

[P L A T E   B]

Second Plate Etched by Seymour

c) The claws holding the globes of the chandelier are close together.

d) Dr. Slammer's watch chain is white. Five buttons show on the right side of his coat. The brim of his hat is straight.

e) The glasses carried by the waiter are shaded.

f) The plate is unsigned by the artist.

a) There are eleven floor boards, the extra one being at the right.

b) Dr. Slammer's left foot touches the crack in the floor. Jingle's left foot is nearer the crack than in the first plate, while his right heel crosses the edge of the second step.

c) The claws holding the lamp globes are farther apart.

d) Slammer's watch chain is white. Five and a half buttons show on the right side of his coat. The brim of his hat shows a distinct curve so that it nearly covers his right eye.

e) The glasses carried by the waiter are not shaded.

f) The plate is unsigned.

In the second state of this plate the apron of the waiter, where it shows between the posts of the balcony, is shaded, and diagonal shade lines have been added between the lower balcony posts.

Dr. Slammer's defiance of Jingle

[PLATE C]

Copy of Seymour's Plate Etched by Browne for the 1838 Edition

a) There are eleven floor boards.

b) Slammer's and Jingle's feet are as in Plate B.

c) As in Plate B.

d) Slammer's watch chain is black, and the brim of his hat is curved.

e) As in Plate B.

f) The plate is unsigned, but the legend *Dr. Slammer's defiance of Jingle* has been added.

Part I · Plate 5 · Page 31

The Dying Clown

After Seymour's unfortunate experience with soft steel plates for his first four etchings, he obtained better material; consequently, no duplicates were made by him of the next three. They were, however, copied by Browne for the bound volume of 1838 with legends below the pictures.

The letter which has often been spoken of as having been the cause of Seymour's despondency and the ending of his connection with *Pickwick*, is now in the Widener Collection at Harvard University. Dickens wrote, April 14, 1836, in part as follows:

"I am extremely anxious about 'The Stroller's Tale,' the more especially as many literary friends on whose judgment I place great reliance, think it will create considerable sensation. I have seen your design for an etching to accompany it. I think it extremely good, but still, it is not my idea; and as I feel so very solicitous to have it as complete as possible, I shall feel personally obliged to you if you will make another drawing. It will give me great pleasure to see you, as well as the drawing, when it is complete. With this view, I have asked Chapman and Hall to take a glass of grog with me on Sunday evening (the only night I am disengaged), when I hope you will be able to look in.

"The alterations I want, I will endeavour to explain. I think the woman should be younger, the 'Dismal man' decidedly should, and he should be less miserable in appearance. To communicate an interest to the plate, his whole appearance should express more sympathy and solicitude; and while I represent the sick man as emaciated and dying, I would not make him too repulsive. The furniture of the room, you have depicted *admirably*."

The last sentence is damning with faint praise.

page 31

[P L A T E   A]

Etched by Seymour

a) The plate is signed *Seymour, Del.* in the lower left margin.
b) The foot of the listener touches the hat on the floor.
c) The cup on the mantel is poorly etched and shows broken lines.
d) There are clothes drying on a cord before the fireplace.
e) The pitcher on the shelf at the right is unshaded.
f) There is a white space between the two hands of the woman.

[P L A T E   B]

Copied by Browne after Seymour for the 1838 Edition

a) The signature is *Seymour*, but the Greek ε and the final capital *E* show it to be Browne's etching. There is an inscription below the drawing, *The dying Clown*.
b) The hat on the floor is separated some distance from the foot of the listener.
c) The cup on the mantel is complete.
d) There are no clothes in front of the fireplace.
e) The pitcher on the shelf at the right is shaded.
f) The fingers of the woman's hands touch.

The dying Clown.

London, Chapman & Hall, 186 Strand.

Mr. Pickwick in Chase of His Hat

This plate also was etched only once by Seymour and only once copied by Browne. There are slight signs of retouching in both.

[PLATE A]

Etched by Seymour

a) The signature in the lower center is clearly in Seymour's hand. Below it only the page number is given.
b) The lady in the carriage back of the fat boy has feathers in her hat, and there are no stitches shown on the backs of her gloves.
c) The woman on top of the carriage in the rear has her eyes almost concealed by shadows.
d) There is one less face in the doorway of the carriage than in the second plate.
e) The man at the extreme right of the plate is very faintly etched.
f) There are apparently fifteen spokes in the carriage wheel.
g) A lock of hair at Mr. Snodgrass' left is blowing almost horizontally to the right.

[PLATE B]

Copied from the Seymour Plate by Browne for the 1838 Edition

a) There is no signature. The engraved title is *Mr. Pickwick in chase of his hat.*
b) The lady back of the fat boy has no feathers in her hat, and there are three rows of stitches in the back of her glove.
c) The woman in the second carriage shows part of her forehead.
d) There is one more face in the carriage door than in the preceding plate.
e) The man at the extreme right of the plate is clearly seen.
f) There are but fourteen spokes in the wheel.
g) Mr. Snodgrass' stray lock of hair droops at an angle of 45°.

page.38

Mr Pickwick in chase of his hat.

Mr. Winkle Soothes the Refractory Steed

This plate was etched only once by Seymour and later copied by Browne.

[P L A T E A]

Original Plate by Seymour

a) The plate is signed in the lower center, *Seymour, Del* in script.
b) The refractory horse's ears point upward at an angle, the saddle is without a raised piece in front, and the stirrup is swung forward.
c) The horse attached to the four-wheeled chaise has only one rein; its ears slope somewhat backward, giving it an appearance of astonishment.
d) Mr. Winkle's leggings have buttons shown as small circles.
e) The whip at Mr. Winkle's feet has a handle defined only by two lines.
f) The background is lightly engraved.
g) Below the plate appears only *page 47.*

[P L A T E B]

Copied from the Seymour Plate by Browne for the 1838 Edition

a) The plate is signed *Seymour, del* with "Phiz's" typical δ in *del*, showing clearly that it is not a re-etching by Seymour.
b) The ears of the horse in the foreground point farther back than in the earlier plate, the saddlebow is raised in front in the place where in a Western saddle the pommel occurs, and the stirrup hangs down, although the strap to which it is attached is still swung forward, but it is somewhat hard to see on account of the shading of the bellyband.
c) The horse attached to the chaise has two reins, its ears are more nearly vertical than in the preceding, so that the horse has an amused look.
d) Mr. Winkle's legging buttons are shown as black dots.
e) The whip handle is made up of three lines.
f) The background as well as the whole plate is more heavily etched.
g) The page number no longer occurs, but the plate is inscribed *Mr. Winkle soothes the refractory steed.*

Mr. Winkle soothes the refractory steed

London, Chapman & Co & Wi. Strike.

The Cricket Match

Original and only plate. After the death of Seymour, April 20, 1836, Robert W. Buss was employed to take his place. He etched Plates 8 and 9 for Part III, but they were very unsatisfactory, and in October, 1836, Browne etched two substitute plates. The first of the Buss plates is signed at the lower left *Drawn & Etch'd by R. W. Buss*, the letter *R* in his name is reversed, so that the first stroke of the *W* forms its upright. This plate was never etched in duplicate, but it was retouched so that it exists in several states, distinguished chiefly by the strengthening of the background figures. Since in this book we are concerned only with the "Phiz" plates, no illustrations of the several states are given, the one shown here being sufficient for the completion of the *Pickwick* series.

When Browne in October, 1836, etched two new plates as substitutes for the Buss plates, he did not use "The Cricket Match" as a subject. He chose in its place a more interesting scene which was inserted on page 76 and had as its engraved title *Mr. Wardle and his friends under the influence of the salmon.* In this book it is described as Plate 9*A*.

The reason for Dickens' dissatisfaction with the Buss plates is perfectly clear, for, while etchings by Buss for other books are infinitely better than these two for Dickens, the latter are very crude and amateurish. Not only are the drawings bad, but the etching is poorly done. One might excuse the workmanship as due to inexperience in handling a new medium, but the drawings are so childish that in those days before childish drawings were

Drawn & Etch'd by RWBuss.

Page 69

The Fat Boy Awake on This Occasion Only

Drawn & Etch'd by RWBuss

Page 74

fashionable and considered good art it is surprising that an artist would have the courage to submit them to the publishers. The acceptance by Chapman and Hall, of course, was Hobson's choice and due to the immediate need for plates for Part III. It is fortunate that Buss was not further engaged.

Etched by Buss

As mentioned under Plate 8, Buss etched two plates which were later replaced by two by Browne. The second Buss plate, often spoken of as "The Arbour Scene," is signed in the lower

page 73

center *Drawn & Etch'd by R. W. Buss* and *Page 74.* It was not etched in duplicate, although there are several states, chiefly distinguished by a strengthening of the lines and a darkening of the whole plate. Since it is not by Browne, only an example of the first state is given, characterized by the clear-cut cross-ruling of Mr. Tupman's and the fat boy's coats and of the latter's left trouser leg. The drawing is terrible.

[P L A T E B]

Replacement Plate Etched by Browne

It is hardly fair to compare Buss's etchings for Plates 8 and 9 with Browne's substitute plates, for while Buss's were his first attempts, the Browne substitutes were actually etched after he had already been working on *Pickwick* for about three months. Buss's plates should be compared with Browne's first plate, "The Breakdown," which itself was not too successful but was much better than the one by Buss.

Browne's drawing is beautifully done, and it and Plate 9*A* compare very favorably with much of his subsequent work. In fact, one might almost say that Browne tried himself in these two etchings. They show none of the hurried work of some of his later drawings. The whole design of Plate 9 was changed and greatly improved. The figures are smaller, and there is a house in the background. It is signed in the lower center *Phiz, del.*, the *d* resembling a *b* or a Greek δ. There is no need for discussing differences between this plate and Buss's, for there is no resemblance. There was no second steel by Browne. When the plate was used for the bound volume in 1838, the page number below the design was removed and the legend *The fat boy awake on this occasion only* was added.

page 76

Part III · Plate 9✷ · Page 76

Mr. Wardle and His Friends under the Influence of the Salmon

This etching was substituted for the first Buss plate. It is a beautiful piece of work in design, humor, and as an etching. The shocked faces of the family as contrasted with the amusement

shown by the servants are exceedingly well done, and the sub-dual of the background shows an excellent piece of etching.

The early impressions of this plate show the signature *Phiz, del.* at the lower center, and below it and to the right *page 76*. Later the same plate was used in the bound volume of 1838 with the legend *Mr. Wardle and his friends under the influence of the salmon* added. It was etched only once.

Part IV · Plate 10 · Page 89

The Breakdown

This engraving is very confusing and much less successful than the two preceding "Phiz" plates, which, however, while preceding in the book, actually were etched later than Plate 10. Browne himself probably realized this confused drawing, for he made some drastic changes when he drew a new design for the revised plate used in the bound volume of 1838. But even the new drawing is not too good. For this and the following plate, Browne took the pseudonym "N.E.M.O.," but thereafter he used "Phiz"; perhaps, after the success of the Weller plate, he became "someone" instead of "no one."

In the descriptions of some of the preceding plates, the pro-gressive changes produced by retouching were mentioned. Per-haps Plate 10 is as good an example as any for showing what happened in one case, for they are very noticeable here.

[P L A T E A₁]

First State

a) The artist's signature is *N.E.M.O.* in very faint letters in the lower left corner. If the steel was at all worn or the plate chemically cleaned, it may not show at all. It appears in the original here reproduced but may not appear in the reproduction.

Plate 9✷ PICKWICK / 19

page 89

page 89

b) There are but three horses shown with the wreck of Pickwick's chaise.

c) The wheel on the ground shows the two down-pointing spokes ending short of the felly.

d) The felly itself is rather sketchy.

e) The dark part of Jingle's chaise is shaded only by vertical lines.

f) Wardle's fist appears adjacent to his head.

g) There is no hat between the foot of Pickwick's postboy and the white horse.

h) The postillion at the right has a white jacket.

i) There is no legend below the design but only the words *page 89*.

a) The signature *N.E.M.O.* is very faint.

b) Same as first state.

c) The spokes have been repaired.

d) The felly has been redrawn so that the inner line is unbroken.

e) Same as first state.

f) Same as first state.

g) Same as first state.

h) Same as first state.

i) Same as first state.

page 89

[P L A T E A₃]

Third State

a) The signature has almost disappeared.
b) Same as first state.
c) Same as second state.
d) The felly has been redrawn, so that both upper and lower lines of the lower part are definitely defined. There are also a few lines added running parallel with the rim.
e) Diagonal shade lines have been added to the dark part of Jingle's carriage.
f–i) Same as first state.

The Breakdown

[P L A T E B]

Etched for the Bound Volume of 1838

a) The signature, now *Phiz, del.*, appears at the lower center.

b) There are now four horses in the foreground, and their positions have been changed.

c–d) The wheel on the ground is no longer there.

e) The dark part of Jingle's chaise is again shaded only with vertical lines. The front horse of this chaise is white, and the postboy riding it wears a stovepipe hat instead of a cap.

f) Wardle's arm is uplifted, and he himself is standing up straighter, so that the side of his face shows.

g) There is now a second hat on the ground.

h) The postboy at the right has a striped jacket.

i) The page number has been removed, and the legend *The breakdown* has been engraved below the etching.

Part IV · Plate 11 · Page 94

First Appearance of Mr. Samuel Weller

With the appearance of Sam Weller in the story, the sales of the parts leaped upward. This must have been due entirely to the story itself and not to the "Phiz" drawing, for Sam's appearance hardly gave promise of any future remarkable brilliancy. The 1838 plate is somewhat more successful. There are many differences between the original plate and the replacement, too many to list and unnecessary, for the fact that the second has an engraved legend is in itself sufficient to separate them. A few points of dissimilarity may be mentioned.

[P L A T E A₁]

First State

a) The signature *N.E.M.O.* in the lower right corner is very faint.

b) There is no legend below the design but only the page number.

c) The boots at the extreme lower left are very sketchy and faint and hardly recognizable as boots.

d) Wardle's cane shows a break in the middle, the two parts being tied together by a single line at the left.

e) The buttons on Pickwick's vest are on the wrong side of the line.

page 94

First appearance of Mr Samuel Weller

[P L A T E A₂]

Second State

The only essential changes made in retouching this plate were the repairing
of Wardle's cane and the redrawing of the boots in the lower left corner.

[P L A T E B]

Used in the Bound Volume for 1838

a) The signature is now *Phiz, del* at the lower center.

b) There is no page number, but there is the legend *First appearance of Mr. Samuel Weller.* Below that, as usual, there are the publishers' name and address.

c) The boots have decreased in number but are well drawn. They are quite differently placed from those in the preceding plates.

d) Wardle's left hand shows, his cane is smoother, and his coattails show on both sides of his legs. His trousers are white.

e) There are no buttons on Pickwick's vest.

There are many other changes, for the entire drawing was new. There is only one sign on the van cover, and the inscription is readable. The man who was partly hidden by the cover in the first plate is now shown more fully. The dog at Pickwick's feet is more white than black. The landlady wears an apron, and there is a birdcage in front of her. There are three instead of four men in the doorway at the back. There is no man on the bundle back of Mr. Pickwick.

Part V · Plate 12 · Page 117

Mrs. Bardell Faints in Mr. Pickwick's Arms

The original plate illustrating the main cause of Mr. Pickwick's woe is rather washed out in appearance, but it was much improved in the second etching. Only two plates were made: the original one which accompanied Part V of the parts and which was several times retouched, especially to strengthen the lines of all the faces, and the one with the engraved legend which appeared in the bound volume of 1838. In the first plate **Mr.** Tupman's satisfaction at having a comeback for his own earlier amatory defection is clearly shown, but Snodgrass and Winkle show their dismay. In Plate 12-B Snodgrass and Winkle as well as Tupman show their *Schadenfroheit.*

page 117.

[P L A T E A₁]

a) The first appearance of the new signature *Phiz, del* is at the bottom of the etching, somewhat to the left of the center. Below this, near the center, are the words *page 117.*

b) There are several bell jars on the mantel covering ornaments, but no clock. There are no vases at the sides.

c) Mr. Winkle's legs are straight.

d) Snodgrass' feet are together, and his right hand is across his breast.

e) Tommy is kicking Mr. Pickwick with his left foot.

f) There is a small landscape on the wall above the mirror.

g) Mr. Pickwick has a firm grip around Mrs. Bardell's waist, but he is standing.

page 117.

Mrs. Bardell faints in Mr. Pickwick's arms.

Etched Later for the 1838 Bound Volume

a) The artist's signature is clear cut. The page number has been omitted, but the legend *Mrs. Bardell faints in Mr. Pickwick's arms*, as well as the publishers' name and address, has been engraved below.

[P L A T E   A₂]

In the retouched plate all lines of the figures and especially of the faces are strengthened.

b) The single bell jar on the mantel covers a clock, and there are vases at the ends.

c) Winkle's knees are bent.

d) Snodgrass' right hand appears above Tupman's back, and his feet are not together.

e) Tommy Bardell is kicking Pickwick with his right foot.

f) The picture above the mirror is quite large and strongly etched. It shows Cupid and a girl.

g) Mrs. Bardell seems to have been sitting on Pickwick's lap, but, upon the opening of the door, he has somewhat relaxed his embrace.

page 132

Part V · Plate 13 · Page 132

The Election at Eatonswill

Two plates were etched: the original one which appeared in the novel as it came out in parts and the re-etched plate for the bound volume of 1838. The first plate was retouched, but the changes are unimportant and consist chiefly in strengthening the shadows. Both plates are crowded, but, while the original one is confusing, the one with the engraved inscription gives only the feeling of a rioting crowd. It is decidedly the better of the two.

[P L A T E A₁]

a) The signature *Phiz, del* and *page 132* appear below the design.

b) The beadle's legs are straight, and his staff, faintly etched, reaches above the head of the man in the background.

c) The trousers of the man with the sign in the lower left corner show only vertical stripes.

d) There are no horizontal lines of shading below the balcony.

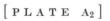

page 132

The Election at Eatanswill.

[P L A T E A₂]

In the retouched plate, the beadle's staff is quite distinct, the trousers of the man with the sign are checked, and the shadows below the balcony have been strengthened by horizontal lines.

[P L A T E B]

Etched Later for the 1838 Bound Volume

a) The artist's signature is very faint, below and to the left of the end of the wooden leg. An inscription, *The election at Eatonswill* and the publishers' name and address take the place of the page number below the design.

b) The beadle's legs are bowed, and his feet are far apart. His staff is short and hardly reaches the chin of the man behind.

c) The man with the sign in the lower left corner now has white trousers and a cockade on his hat. He is certainly not Sam Weller, as Miller and Strange assert.

d) The floor of the balcony is for the greater part behind the signs carried by the mob.

Part VI · Plate 14 · Page 154

Mrs. Leo Hunter's Fancy-Dress Dejeune

The page numbers below the designs in this and the following plate were inadvertently transposed, and a few copies of Plate 14 bear the page number 169 and a few of Plate 15 bear 154. These errors were soon corrected, and plates with the incorrect numbers are the rarest of all Pickwick plates. The corrected plates in most cases show traces of the original numbers. Since the drawing itself was not affected, it is incorrect to speak of the corrected plates as revisions. The plate with the engraved legend, however, is entirely new.

[P L A T E   A]

a) The signature *Phiz, del* and *page 154* appear in the lower center.

b) Count Smorltork has no mustache, and the front of his chin is bare, but he has ample whiskers beneath it.

c) A birdcage rests high up among the branches of the tree.

d) Mr. Tupman's legs are straight and his knees together. He has no feathers in his hat.

e) There is a small pool of water in the foreground.

f) The girl in the background at the left has her hand near her mouth, which is open in astonishment or amusement.

page 154

[PLATE B]

Etched Later for the 1838 Bound Volume

a) The page number is missing, but there is a legend *Mrs. Leo Hunter's fancy-dress dejeune* and the publishers' name and address engraved at the bottom.

b) Count Smorltork has a full beard.
c) The birdcage hangs from the lowest branch of the tree.
d) Mr. Tupman's legs are bent, and his knees are separated. There are two feathers in his hat.
e) The pool is missing from the foreground.
f) The girl at the left, back of Mrs. Leo Hunter, has her mouth closed.

Part VI · Plate 15 · Page 169

The Unexpected Breaking-Up of the Seminary for Young Ladies

A few copies of this plate were issued with incorrect pagination, as mentioned under Plate 14, but no changes were made in the design when this was corrected. A bolt on the door near the top was marked for deletion, but this was overlooked when the plate was printed. The first plate shows sketchily drawn young girls in the doorway, while in the second they are older and well done. The facial expressions are better in the second plate except those of Mr. Pickwick and the cook. In the first plate his face shows better Pickwick's horror at his predicament.

[PLATE A]

a) "Phiz's" signature is to the right of the lower center. The page number is nearly central.
b) There are six bolts showing on the door, one of them marked for deletion. The "lady abbess" had certainly made sure that that door could not be opened from the outside!
c) There is no bell on the hook in the center of the door.
d) There are seventeen teachers, maids, and pupils shown, some of them barely discernible.
e) The cook's skirt is white near the top.

[PLATE B]

Etched Later for the 1838 Bound Volume

a) "Phiz's" signature is at the lower center. The page number has disappeared, and a legend has been engraved below the design.

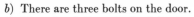

page 169

b) There are three bolts on the door.

c) There is a bell on the hook in the center of the door.

d) There are thirteen clearly drawn teachers, pupils, and maids in the doorway.

e) The cook's skirt is shaded all over.

Mr. Pickwick in the Pound

The original plate and that prepared for the bound volume of 1838 show decided differences. Artistically, there is not much choice between them.

[PLATE A]

a) The signature, *Phiz*, *del*. and *page 197* are shown below the design.
b) There are two donkeys (exclusive of Mr. Pickwick) in the pound, but the hind legs of the larger donkey are very lightly sketched, so that they have been described as missing. In spite of that, she—I suppose it is a she—can smile at Mr. Pickwick.
c) The windows in the gables of the houses, right and left, are closed.
d) There is but one child peering through the bars at the right, above Mr. Pickwick's left foot.
e) The two men at the extreme left have no bodies.
f) The head of the rake in the hands of the boy immediately in front of the left corner post is very indistinct, and in most prints only the handle shows and appears like a staff.
g) The chimney sweep's cap is black.

[PLATE B]

Etched Later for the 1838 Bound Volume

a) The legend and publishers' imprint replace the page number below the design.
b) Only the lady donkey remains in the pound. She is showing her teeth.
c) The windows in the gables of the two houses are half-open.
d) There are two children peeping between the bars above Mr. Pickwick's left foot.
e) A body has been added to the man at the left.
f) The rake in the hands of the boy is clearly shown.
g) The chimney sweep's cap is white.

page 197.

Mr. Pickwick in the Pound.

London, Chapman & Hall, 186 Strand.

Mr. Pickwick and Sam in the Attorney's Office

Although redrawn, the plate with the engraved legend differs only slightly from the original. Neither is very good, but the original is somewhat the better of the two, especially in the various facial expressions.

[PLATE A₁]

a) The signature *Phiz, del.* and *page 201* appear below the design.
b) Sam Weller's knees are close together.
c) The third law clerk from the left has no pen in his hand.
d) The half-door leading to the clerks' room is shaded only in the lower right corner. It has no knob.
e) The vertical shading of the inside of the top shelf of the bookcase at the left and the shading of the end of the case at the right do not extend all the way to the top.
f) The bars between the windowpanes which appear between the second and third clerks, as well as the horizontal bars, are shown by broken lines.
g) The poster on the partition has ten columns of print.

[PLATE A₂]

In the second state of this plate the shading within the bookshelves has been extended entirely to the top, the panels on the door have been completed, and the shading has been extended upward. The window bars have been drawn out in full.

Etched Later for the 1838 Bound Volume

a) Below the signature the plate is inscribed *Mr. Pickwick & Sam in the attorneys' office.*
b) Sam Weller's knees are apart.
c) The third clerk has a quill pen in his hand.
d) The door is shaded much like the second state of Plate A, but it now has a knob.
e) The bookcases are shaded with lines in two directions.
f) The window bars are complete except that they do not quite join at the corners.
g) The poster has nine columns of print.

Part VIII · Plate 18 · Page 223

The Last Visit of Heyling to the Old Man

An unattractive subject, unattractively drawn.

[P L A T E   A]

a) Below the design, somewhat to the right of the center, is the signature *Phiz, del* in rather thin and pale letters, and below it *page 223*.
b) Above Heyling's shoulders the knobs at the top of the back of the chair show.
c) The legs and the braces of the old man's chair are turned. The back extends above his head.
d) The old man's face is in profile.
e) There are three ceiling joists, not counting the one at the back against the wall of the room.

page.223

The last visit of Heyling to the old man

[P L A T E   B]

Etched Later for the 1838 Bound Volume

a) The artist's signature is nearly in the lower center. The page number has been omitted and the words *The last visit of Heyling to the old man* have been engraved in the lower margin.

b) The top of Heyling's chair does not show.

c) The legs and braces of the old man's chair are square. The back reaches only to his eyes.

d) The old man's face is turned so that both eyes show.

e) There are but two ceiling joists, excluding the one against the wall of the room.

Part VIII · Plate 19 · Page 233

The Middle-aged Lady in the Double-bedded Room

Owing to the scattered patches of light and shade, the picture is inartistic by lacking a central point of interest, and one's eyes wander. There seems to have been no retouching of the original plate, and all copies seen are alike even to the smallest details.

[PLATE A]

a) *Phiz, del* is very faintly engraved near the lower center, and *page 233* somewhat to the right of it.
b) The chair in the center of the picture is very dark, and it has three vertical bars.
c) The cap on the chair is white and the dress black.
d) The lamp shade on the floor has only eight light spots.
e) The lock on the door is clearly defined.
f) The middle-aged lady has lifted her back hair above the horizontal.

[PLATE B]

Etched Later for the 1838 Bound Volume

a) The signature is strong and has flourishes in front and behind. The page number has been replaced by the legend *The middle-aged lady in the double bedded room.* The publishers' imprint is below.
b) The chair in the center is light colored and shows crossed bars.
c) The cap on the chair is light colored and the dress is a white nightgown.
d) The lamp on the floor has fourteen or more light spots.
e) The door lock is lost in the confused dark background.
f) The lady's back hair is being held out horizontally. She is younger and better looking than in Plate A.

page 233

The middle aged lady in the double bedded room

London, Chapman & Hall, 186 Strand.

Mr. Weller Attacks the Executive of Ipswich

This is a good plate, with well-balanced light and shade and a strong central point of interest. It was apparently never re-touched, for all copies show the same shade lines without additions. There is not a great deal of difference between the original and the plate with the engraved title, but the middle-distance figures are more pronounced in outline in the latter.

[PLATE A]

a) There is no face on the signboard at the right.
b) Mr. Pickwick's thumb is turned in.
c) The man behind Mr. Snodgrass shows three-fourths front view and has his hat pulled down over his eyes. His hand and one leg show. The man behind him looks like a fox terrier.
d) The man on horseback has his mouth open.
e) Sam Weller's hat is white.
f) One of the men in the window of the inn at the right has a pipe in his hand.
g) Sam Weller's mouth is turned up in a smile.
h) "Phiz's" signature is small in the lower center. The page number is farther to the right.

[PLATE B]

Etched Later for the 1838 Bound Volume

a) There is a face on the signboard at the right.
b) Mr. Pickwick's thumb is turned out.
c) The man behind Snodgrass shows his profile, and his body is not well defined. The man behind him is much clearer than before.
d) The man on horseback has his mouth closed, and he is smiling.
e) Sam's hat is dark with a white band.
f) The man in the window of the inn has no pipe.
g) Sam Weller's mouth is turned down.
h) The artist's signature looks like "Ring, del." There is no page number. The legend is *Mr. Weller attacks the executive of Ipswich.*

page 251

Mr Weller attacks the executioner of Ipswich.

London Chapman & Hall, 186 Strand.

Part IX · Plate 21 · Page 265

Job Trotter Encounters Sam in Mr. Muzzle's Kitchen

Again the first plate shows no signs of retouching in the later impressions, and not until the second plate was etched for the bound volume, was there any variation in the prints.

[PLATE A]

a) The artist's signature is at the lower center, and the page number is somewhat farther to the right.

b) The kitten on the stool is not very clearly drawn, and the cat—or is it a dog?—on the floor is part white and part black.

c) The hands of the clock indicate ten minutes to twelve.

d) There are only three items on the lower shelf of the china closet.

e) There is a ladle in the kettle on the fire.

f) Only the ends of the fingers of Sam's left hand show.

[PLATE B]

Etched Later for the 1838 Bound Volume

a) The signature is in the lower center, and below it are the legend *Job Trotter encounters Sam in Mr. Muzzle's kitchen* and the publishers' imprint.

b) The animal on the floor near the stool looks decidedly like a dog. It is black except for white feet and white patches in front.

c) There is but one hand on the clock, or else it is exactly twelve.

d) The lower shelf has a long row of plates.

e) There is no ladle in the soup kettle.

f) Sam's whole hand shows at Mary's waist.

The faces of all the characters except Job have pleasanter expressions in the first plate than in the second.

page 265

Job Trotter encounters Sam in Mr. Muzzle's kitchen.

London, Chapman & Hall, 186, Strand.

Part X · Plate 22 · Page 296

Christmas Eve at Mr. Wardle's

Beginning with this plate, Browne began to etch duplicate designs on quarto steel plates instead of attempting to retouch the originals. The two are practically identical, and since they were printed simultaneously and later cut apart, it is incorrect to say that either is the original one. One, of course, was etched before the other, but it is not always possible to say which that was. In the following descriptions, the one to which the engraved title was later added is considered the second, and this one with the engraved title is considered the third. Incidentally, copies with the engraved titles are more difficult to obtain than bound volumes without them. Since the second and third plates were actually printed from the same steels, usually only one is illustrated in the following pages.

All the plates show Mr. Pickwick wearing gaiters, although Dickens said (p. 293): "If any thing could have added to the interest of this agreeable scene [the Christmas Eve party], it would have been the remarkable fact of Mr. Pickwick's appearing without his gaiters, for the first time within the memory of his oldest friends."

[P L A T E   A]

a) The signature *Phiz* is in fairly large script in the lower middle. The page number is farther to the right.
b) The foreground shows a cat and a pug dog, and not two cats, as said by Miller and Strange.

page 296

[PLATE B₁]

page 296

c) The front rafter shows two strings of onions, a side of bacon, and three hams suspended from it, and there are festoons of evergreens and mistletoe connecting them.

d) The girl with Winkle has her face turned so that only her profile shows. The one with Tupman has flowers in her hair.

e) The fireplace is seen from the side.

f) The head of the girl to the right of Sam Weller is not very near his.

g) **Mr. Pickwick's** legs are not crossed, and there is no cat between him and the old lady.

a) "Phiz's" signature is smaller. The *g* of *page* ends in a downstroke, while in the first plate it forms a loop.

b) There is neither cat nor dog in the foreground.

c) There are more provisions on the rafter than before, but there is no festoon. The bunch of mistletoe remains.

d) Winkle's girl shows her full face, and Snodgrass' has a black ribbon or bun of hair on her head.

e) The fireplace is seen more from the front, so that the left side does not show.

Christmas Eve at Mr Wardle's

London, Chapman & Hall, 186 Strand.

f) The head of the girl back of Sam is very close to his.

g) Mr. Pickwick's legs are crossed, and there is a cat between him and old Mrs. Wardle.

This is not a new plate but is Plate B₁ upon which has been engraved the inscription *Christman Eve at Mr. Wardle's.*

Part X · Plate 23 · Page 301

The Goblin and the Sexton

Miller and Strange say that the earliest impressions of this plate show no page number, while Hatton and Cleaver regard plates with missing pagination as proof impressions before the page numbers were added. I have a copy with the page number almost obliterated by wear, so that if the position were not known, it might very easily be overlooked.

This plate is very well done, although it has hardly the appearance of being "in the pale moonlight."

[PLATE A]

a) The tree back of the sexton shows a face near his head.
b) There is no tombstone to the right of the sexton's left foot.
c) The signature *Phiz, del* is faint and lies partly in the grass.
d) There is no finial at the apex of the roof of the church.
e) There is a bone between the lantern and the sexton's feet.
f) The highest branch of the tree at the right is lower in the drawing than the roof of the tower in the background.

[PLATE B₁]

a) The tree has a knot where the face was in Plate A.
b) There is a tombstone at the right of the sexton's left foot.
c) The artist's signature is clear and lies below the grass.
d) There is a round finial at the apex of the roof.

page.301

page.301

e) There is a bone between the lantern and the skull but none to the right of the lantern.

f) The upper branch of the tree shows above the church tower in the illustration.

[PLATE B₂]

This is not a new plate but is Plate B₁ with a legend added.

Part XI · Plate 24 · Page 313

Mr. Pickwick Slides

Both the original plate and the duplicate are well balanced, and the etching of the background is excellent. The second plate shows some of the figures in the background a bit more distinctly but not enough to lose the effect of distance.

[PLATE A]

a) The signature in script is rather faint in the lower center; the page number is farther to the right; the figures *313* are not so slanting as the word *page* and seem to have been added later. They are also much fainter.

b) There are four stakes in the ice, with none to the right of Arabella's foot.

c) Mr. Winkle's skates are not shown.

d) The back of Sam Weller's hand rests against his hip.

e) Bob Sawyer's cane is almost white.

f) The dog is mostly black.

g) A church steeple appears on the horizon, and there is one bird in the sky almost directly overhead. A second bird appears dimly over the house at the left, and there is a suggestion of a third at the edge of the clouds at the extreme left.

page 313

d) The palm of Sam Weller's hand rests against his hip.
e) Bob Sawyer's cane is dark.
f) The dog is more white than black.
g) No church steeple appears in the distance. There are four large birds in the sky and seven or eight very small ones over the trees in the background.

[P L A T E B₂]

This plate is from the same steel as Plate B₁, but the page number has been removed, and a legend has been engraved in the lower margin.

Part XI · Plate 25 · Page 326

The First Interview with Mr. Sergeant Snubbin

Exceptionally, the original Plate 25 shows up better than the duplicate. In the latter the ornamentation of the top of the cabinet and the articles piled above stand out so prominently that they lead the eyes away from the center of interest below.

Curiously, in the legend the American spelling "sergeant" is used, while in the text Dickens uses the common English spelling "serjeant" for a lawyer. Similarly, in *Dombey and Son*, the American spelling "parlor" is used in the legend of Plate 31, while the text uses "parlour."

[P L A T E A]

a) The cornice of the cabinet is very slightly ornamented, and on top at the right there are only four books.
b) There is a roll of paper below Sergeant Snubbin's right foot.
c) The jumble of papers on the desk is not well defined.

[P L A T E B₁]

a) The page number *313* is smaller than in Plate A.
b) There are five stakes in the ice, the fifth one to the right of Arabella's fur-topped boots.
c) Mr. Winkle's skates lie beside him.

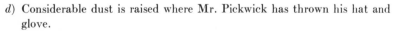

page 326

page 326

d) Considerable dust is raised where Mr. Pickwick has thrown his hat and glove.

e) The artist's signature is near the lower center and is rather faint. The page number is about $\frac{3}{16}$ inch below the signature and halfway between it and the right margin.

[P L A T E B₁]

a) The cornice of the cabinet is heavily ornamented, and there are seven or eight books at the right end.

b) There is no roll of paper at Sergeant Snubbin's foot.

c) The mass of papers on the desk is more clearly defined.

d) There is less dust near Mr. Pickwick's hat.

e) The signature is larger and heavier, and the page number is now about $\frac{3}{8}$ inch below the signature.

[PLATE B₂]

This is not a new plate. The legend has been engraved on Plate B₁ below the design.

Part XII · Plate 26 · Page 343

The Valentine

Beginning with this plate and continuing to the end of the book, there are usually no page numbers but only the artist's signature below the etching. This plate, however, does occur with pagination, not only on Plate A but on Plate B. Miller and Strange, and Hatton and Cleaver think that the plate without the page number is earlier than the one with it, presumably assuming that the page number was etched in afterward. More reasonable is the assumption that, since all the preceding plates had page numbers, this also was at first so etched and that, after the decision was made to omit them thereafter, it was burnished out.

[PLATE A₁]

a) The letter *D* in *Dublin* in the sign on the mantel is reversed.

b) The plate on the mantel at the right behind the pitcher is partly ruled with vertical lines, but there is no face upon it.

c) There is no newspaper on the floor at the right.

d) There is no bowknot at the top of the bell cord.

e) Sam Weller's index finger is on top of the pen, and he holds it as he might in writing. The plume end is against his head.

page 343

f) In the center picture above the mantel, the driver's head touches the inner horizontal line of the frame.

g) There is a picture of a bird on the pitcher behind Tony Weller's arm.

h) The maid behind the screen is more or less faintly etched.

i) The plate has a page number below and to the right of the signature.

[P L A T E A₂]

a–h) Same as Plate A₁.
i) There is no page number in the lower margin.

This is not a new plate but is simply Plate A₁ with the number burnished out.

[P L A T E B₁]

a) The letter *D* in *Dublin* is broken, but it can hardly be said to have been corrected, as Miller and Strange assert. The word is incomplete, the final *in* being replaced by dots. The *E* of *Guinness* lacks the vertical stroke, but the position of the middle bar shows that this letter also was reversed.

b) The plate on the mantel at the right shows a face.

c) There is a newspaper on the floor below the chair at the right.

d) There is a bowknot at the top of the bell cord.

e) Sam holds his pen in his fist with the plume toward the left, and he appears to be scratching his head with the nib.

f) The driver in the central picture over the mantel is seated lower than before, so that there is quite a clear space above his head.

g) The pitcher behind Tony's elbow has no decoration.

h) The maid behind the screen, especially her head, is more sharply defined than in Plate A.

i) There is a page number in the lower margin.

[P L A T E   B₂]

a) This plate is the same as Plate B₁ except that the page number has been removed.

[P L A T E   B₃]

To Plate B₂ the legend *The Valentine* has been added. It was printed from the same steel as Plates B₁ and B₂ but appeared only in the bound volume of 1838.

Part XII · Plate 27 · Page 358

The Trial

This plate, like the preceding, occurs with or without page numbers, but hereafter the numbers are missing from all the plates. Neither design is particularly artistic. Sergeant Buzfuz is too large for the other characters, and Mr. Perker, while described as a little man, is too small when compared with his size as shown in other plates, e.g., in his first meeting with Sam Weller.

[P L A T E   A₁]

a) The most easily recognizable characteristic of this plate is the absence of Mr. Perker's hat behind him.

page 358.

b) The papers on the floor beneath Perker's feet are not tied.

c) There are only eleven jurymen. The third from the left wears glasses.

d) Mrs. Cluppin has a rather scrawny spray of flowers in her bonnet.

e) There is a page number in the lower margin.

[P L A T E A₂]

This is from the same steel as the preceding, but the page number has been removed.

[P L A T E B₁]

a) Mr. Perker's hat stands behind him on the bench.
b) The papers on the floor below Perker's feet are tied.

c) There are twelve jurymen. The third from the left has no glasses.

d) Mrs. Cluppin's bonnet now has a ribbon and a small feather.

e) There is a page number in the lower margin.

Hatton and Cleaver state that Plate B, when it has a page number, is always incorrectly marked *page 353* instead of "page 358," and that this was never corrected. As a matter of fact, I have a copy with the corrected number.

[P L A T E   B₂]

This is from the same steel as Plate B₁, but the page number has been removed.

[P L A T E   B₃]

This is the plate from the bound volume of 1838. It is from the same steel as B₂ but has had the legend *The Trial* added.

Part XIII · Plate 28 · Page 382

The Card Room at Bath

Beginning with this plate, page numbers were omitted from all the steels, and only the artist's signature appeared below the designs. There is very little difference between each pair of plates, which were engraved together on one steel, printed together, and afterward cut apart. Between the two plates numbered 28, there is very little choice; in each, the heavy ornamental mirrors and chandelier are distracting, and the plates would have been better had they been stopped out sooner while being etched.

[P L A T E   A]

a) The cards on the table in front of Mr. Pickwick are very faintly shown.

b) Pickwick's partner wears a necklace or ruching around the top line of her dress.

47679

c) The tallest man in the background has Lord Dundreary whiskers, and the man at his left with the monocle has his right thumb turned into the palm of his hand.

d) The candles at the side of the mirror at the right clearly show through the shades.

[P L A T E B₂]

This is from the same steel as Plate B₁, but the legend *The Card Room at Bath* has been added.

Part XIII · Plate 29 · Page 391

Mr. Winkle's Situation when the Door Blew To

[P L A T E A]

a) There is a dark area between Mrs. Dowler's left shoulder and her hair.
b) The chairman's hat on the ground is separated from its shadow by a white space.
c) The smoke from the linkboy's torch curves downward.
d) Mr. Winkle's nightcap shows no point.
e) The fat chairman's coat has only six buttons.
f) There is no gap between the cap of the street lamp and its support at the left.
g) The pole on the ground is not shaded at the right end or near the hat.

[P L A T E B₁]

a) Mrs. Dowler's hair reaches her left shoulder.
b) The shadow of the hat in the foreground touches the hat.
c) The smoke of the linkboy's torch curves upward.
d) Mr. Winkle's nightcap has a point.
e) The fat chairman's coat has seven buttons.
f) There is a broken space between the top of the street lamp and its support at the left.
g) The pole on the ground shows a shadow near the hat, and the right end is dark.

[P L A T E B₁]

a) The cards on the table are clearly shown.
b) Mr. Pickwick's partner has only a single line shown at the top of her dress.

Plates 29A and 29B$_1$ PICKWICK / 53

This is Plate B₁ with a legend added.

Part XIV · Plate 30 · Page 409

Conviviality at Bob Sawyer's

Pity the poor patients! Of the two prints for Plate 30, the first one is somewhat the better. Since the scene is laid inside a room, it does not require so much subduing of the background as it would were it outdoors.

[P L A T E A]

a) In the wall case at the left of the door, there is a child's head with hair.
b) A book lies flat on top of the bookshelves at the right.
c) There is no spoon on the floor below the table leg, but there is something which looks like a pill or a cork.
d) The little finger of Bob Sawyer's left hand is extended.
e) The lines of the rim of the mortar are drawn through the pestle.
f) Two of the three cigarettes on the table in front of Winkle are more or less parallel; the third lies across the hinge line of the table leaf.

[P L A T E B₁]

a) The child's head in the wall case has been replaced by a skull.
b) There is no book on top of the bookshelves, but three of the books on the lower shelf lie flat.
c) There is a spoon on the floor.
d) Bob Sawyer's hand is closed firmly on the graduate.
e) The pestle is not divided by the lines of the mortar's rim.
f) The three cigarettes in front of Winkle are practically parallel and at right angles to the curved edge of the table.

[P L A T E B₂]

A legend has been engraved on Plate B₁.

Part XIV · Plate 31 · Page 434

Part XIV · Plate 31 · Page 434

Mr. Pickwick Sits for His Portrait

[PLATE A]

a) Two of the top windowpanes are starred, and the three below have center rings.

b) The clock has but one hand, which points to *VI*, but there is a suggestion of another hand to indicate that the time is ten minutes to six. It cannot be half-past six, as Miller and Strange suggest, for, if so, the hour hand would point halfway between six and seven. Beginning at the top and reading clockwise, the numerals are *XII, XI, X, . . . , V, VI, VII*.

c) The turnkey's coattails show two buttons behind and one on the pocket.

d) The standing fat man facing Mr. Pickwick has two large buttons on the left side of his coat.

e) The mug on the floor has a handle.

f) Sam Weller's coat shows faintly two dark buttons.

[PLATE B₁]

a) There are stars in each of the top windowpanes, but there are no rings in the row below.

b) The clock hands point to seven. The upper figure is reversed and reads *IIX*.

c) The turnkey's coattails show no buttons, but there is one on the pocket.

d) There are three large white buttons on the coat of the fat man facing Mr. Pickwick.

e) The mug on the floor has no handle.

f) Sam's coat shows three white buttons.

[PLATE B₂]

This is Plate B₁ with a legend engraved below.

56 / PICKWICK *Plates 31A and 31B₁*

Part XV · Plate 32 · Page 441

The Warden's Room

[P L A T E   A]

a) The plate is signed *Phiz, del* in the lower middle.
b) Mr. Mivens wears a striped vest.
c) The clothesline shows no loop at the left end.
d) The shirt on the line is lightly shaded within the neckband.
e) The brace at the end of Mr. Pickwick's bed has an enlargement where the bars cross.
f) The poster *Rules for the Fleet Prison* is not badly torn.

[P L A T E   B₁]

a) There is no signature.
b) Mr. Mivens wears a flowered vest.
c) The clothesline shows a loop at the left end.
d) The shirt on the line is very dark within the neckband.
e) The braces of Mr. Pickwick's bed cross without an enlargement.
f) The poster is torn at one corner.

[P L A T E   B₂]

a) A legend is engraved on Plate B₁.

Discovery of Jingle in the Fleet

[P L A T E A]

a) The artist's signature is simply *Phiz*.
b) The countryman at the right has a broken whip in his hand. Part of it is shown by double lines, and it has a straight handle.
c) The two top left windowpanes are incompletely drawn.
d) The plant which the girl is watering has only rudimentary leaves.
e) The mug in Job Trotter's hand has a band around it, and the lid shows clearly.
f) The mug on the floor has two handles.
g) The name *J. Smith* can be distinguished on the window casing.
h) The *Am I not a Man and a Brother* poster extends downward nearly to the mantel.

[P L A T E B₁]

a) The artist's signature is *Phiz, del.*
b) The whip in the hand of the countryman has a hooked handle.
c) The second windowpane is now complete.
d) The girl's plant has more leaves than before.
e) Trotter's mug is plain.
f) The mug on the floor has but a single handle.
g) The lettering on the window casing shows no name but only scattered letters.
h) The poster ends some distance above the mantel.

[P L A T E B₂]

A legend has been engraved on Plate B₁.

Part XVI · Plate 34 · Page 484

The Red-nosed Man Discourseth

The two glass bells over the gas jets are distracting, and the picture would be better without them. The same is true for the heavier shading at the top. Like a stage setting, all the characters face the audience. This is very characteristic of "Phiz's" drawings.

[PLATE A]

a) Sam Weller's chair has turned legs, and there is a cross-brace below Sam's elbows.
b) The buttons of Tony Weller's vest lie along one of the stripes.
c) The right hand of Mr. Stiggins shows the thumb and three fingers, and the bottle in his pocket is rather unobtrusive.
d) There is a hole in the floor below the umbrella.
e) There is a spoon in each of the glasses on the table.
f) There is no spiderweb in the upper left corner of the room.

[PLATE B₁]

a) Same Weller's chair has square legs, and there is no brace in the back.
b) The buttons of Tony Weller's vest lie between two stripes.
c) Mr. Stiggins' right hand shows all the fingers. The bottle in his pocket and the book are clearly shown.
d) There is no hole in the floor.
e) Only one of the glasses has a spoon in it.
f) There is a faint spiderweb in the corner of the room.

[PLATE B₂]

A legend has been added to Plate B₁.

Part XVI · Plate 35 · Page 498

Mrs. Bardell Encounters Mr. Pickwick in the Prison

[PLATE A]

a) There is a handrail at the left of the steps.
b) The riser of the third step from the bottom shows between Mr. Pickwick's coattails.
c) The treads of the steps are shaded.
d) The last two fence bars are unfinished at the lower ends.
e) Sam Weller has a cockade in his hat.
f) A dressed chicken with its toes turned up lies on the ground near the basket in the foreground.

[PLATE B₁]

a) There is no handrail at the side of the steps.
b) The end of the third riser is hidden behind Mr. Pickwick.
c) The treads of the lower two steps are white.
d) The last two bars of the fence are continued downward, to disappear behind Mrs. Cluppin.
e) Sam Weller has no cockade in his hat.
f) There is only a bottle and no chicken near the basket in the foreground.

[PLATE B₂]

A legend has been engraved on Plate B₁.

Mr. Winkle Returns under Extraordinary Circumstances

This is another picture with a background that is disturbing on account of the overabundance of unessentials.

[P L A T E   A]

a) The top shelf against the wall at the right is empty, and the shelf below has books lying flat at the right and left.
b) The top shelf of the cupboard has a bowl and several bottles, and the shelf below has several plates standing upright, a pitcher, and a number of glasses.
c) The back of Mr. Perker's chair is dark.
d) The back of Mr. Pickwick's chair is diced.
e) Winkle's hat is shaded only on the lower side.
f) Arabella's right glove shows stitching on the back.
g) Mary's hat is shaded on both sides.
h) Sam's vest shows no buttons.
i) The middle windowpane in the second row shows no break.

[P L A T E   B₁]

a) There are two bottles on the top shelf but only one flat-lying book on the shelf below.
b) The top shelf of the cupboard has a row of standing plates and a row of glasses, and the shelf below has a decanter and five bottles.
c) The back of Mr. Perker's chair is fairly light.
d) The back of Mr. Pickwick's chair is shaded only by vertical lines.
e) Winkle's hat is shaded on both the upper and the lower sides.
f) Either Arabella's right glove shows no stitching, or else her glove is off.
g) Mary's hat is entirely without shading underneath the brim.
h) Sam's vest shows three buttons.
i) The middle windowpane in the second row shows a number of cracks.

[P L A T E   B₂]

A legend has been added to Plate B₁.

The Ghostly Passengers in the Ghost of a Mail

A very effective and well-balanced plate. The etching of the foreground, the middle distance, and the far distance is perfect. One might wish that the hero and heroine were handsomer, but presumably to the teller of the tale, who is shown at the right and who is decidedly unhandsome, they were sufficiently different. Myself, I would have chosen the girl on top of the other coach!

[PLATE A]

a) The bundle on the ground at the right of the lantern in the foreground is not roped; that at the left shows the rear half of the top unshaded.
b) There is no bundle on top of the principal coach.
c) The bottle below the left foot of the robber with the blunderbuss is dark.
d) The left knob of the crossbar of the claymore is missing or is very small.
e) There are nine buttons on the left side of the vest of the man with the prominent hooked nose at the right.
f) Only one front leg of the horse shows.

[PLATE B₁]

a) The bundle on the ground at the right of the lantern is roped; that at the left is practically dark over the entire top.
b) There is a bundle back of the two outside passengers.
c) The bottle below the foot of the man with the blunderbuss is white.
d) The left knob of the crossbar of the claymore shows.
e) There are only seven buttons on the left side of the vest of the bagman's uncle.
f) Two front legs of the horse show.

[PLATE B₂]

A legend has been added to Plate B₁.

Part XVIII · Plate 38 · Page 533

Mr. Bob Sawyer's Mode of Travelling

In spite of the many persons shown, this is a very satisfactory illustration, as to both drawing and etching. The ragamuffins in the foreground are perhaps a bit too disreputable for the open road beyond Bristol, but the remaining characters live up to Dickens' description.

[P L A T E   A]

a) The Irishman at the right has no bundle tied to his stick.
b) There is but one tassel tied to the flagstaff. The flag itself has traces of a face in the center, but it is almost lost in the shading.
c) The hat of the man with glasses in the passing coach has no tassel and most of the face of the girl next to him shows. The driver's whip crosses above the mouth of the man seated beside him.
d) Pickwick's reading glass does not touch his hand.
e) The boy at the lower left has no shoes.
f) The child lying on the ground shows the side of its face, and its left foot is turned inward.
g) The postboy's coat has two buttons at the back.
h) There is no trace at the side of the white horse.
i) The artist's signature is very small and a little to the left of the center.

[P L A T E   B₁]

a) There is a bundle tied to the stick of the Irishman.
b) There are two tassels below the flag, which now shows a face in the center.
c) The hat of the man with glasses in the passing coach has a tassel; the lower part of the face of the girl beside him is hidden. The driver's whip crosses the passenger's face near his mouth.

d) Pickwick's reading glass touches his hand.
e) The boy at the lower left has a slipper on one foot.
f) The left foot of the child on the ground is turned with the toes down, and her face is concealed.
g) The postboy has no buttons on the back of his coat.
h) A trace extends across the flank of the white horse.
i) "Phiz's" signature is somewhat larger than before and is directly in the center.

Phiz. del.

The Rival Editors

Practically all the actors face the audience.

[PLATE A]

a) Mr. Pott's stockings are white.
b) There is nothing hung on the side of the china cupboard at the right, but at the front there are three pitchers suspended from the top board.
c) The birdcage shows but little of the bird.
d) The bird at the top of the clock is black.
e) The fire shovel has an oval knob at the end.
f) The artist's signature at the left of the center is very small.
g) There is no mug on the table between Sam's feet.
h) The top of the middle chair is entirely shaded with parallel lines.
i) The overturned chair at the right shows a white disk in the center of the back. The brace at the right does not touch it.

[PLATE B₁]

a) Mr. Pott's stockings are black.
b) The china cupboard has a jug and a toasting fork hung at the side, and at the front five jugs (or mugs or pitchers) hang from the top.
c) More of the bird in the cage is shown than before.
d) The bird at the top of the clock is almost white.
e) The fire shovel in Mr. Pott's hand has a round knob at the end.
f) The artist's signature is larger and near the bottom center.
g) There is a mug on the table between Sam's calves.
h) The top of the middle chair is only half-shaded.
i) The overturned chair shows a black center in the disk, and the back brace touches it at the side.

[PLATE B₂]

A legend has been engraved on Plate B₁.

[PLATE B₂]

A legend has been etched on Plate B₁.

Plate 38 B₁ PICKWICK / 67

Mary and the Fat Boy

Hatton and Cleaver (p. 21) say that Plates 40 and 41 were etched in triplicate and that this point has never previously been recorded. They then give the points distinguishing the three:

1st. The knife in the Fat Boy's hand points downwards.

2d. The knife points upwards. The back of chair behind Mary is fully shaded, and artist's signature varies from the third plate.

3d. The knife points upwards. The top rail of chair is unshaded.

I disagree not only in not considering the third plate a new one but with the order of the plates. Prints from all three are here given. Plate A is correct as No. 1 above. I would, however, make Hatton and Cleaver's third plate the second, and the second the third, since the engraved title was later engraved upon the one marked "2d" above, which is my Plate B_2.

While there are the following slight variations between Plates B_1 and B_2, the changes are only such as might have been made in retouching a worn plate. Even the signature, being near the edge of the engraving, would have been quickly worn and re-engraved. The fainter lines of the retouched Plate B_2 are identical with the shade lines of the original B_1.

[P L A T E A]

a) The fat boy's knife points downward.

b) There is a saltcellar on the table between the knife and the tumbler, and the pitcher is not shaded on the left side.

c) Both the chairs back of Mary have round-topped backs.

d) Mary's apron pocket is distinctly seen, and her slippers show straps crossed over her ankles.

[PLATE B₁]

a) The fat boy's knife points upward.
b) There is no saltcellar on the table, and the mug back of the meat pie is dark.
c) Only the nearest of the two chairs back of Mary has a round-topped back, but both of them are unshaded.
d) Mary's pocket hardly shows, and her slippers have no crossed straps.
e) The braces connecting the legs of the fat boy's chair are white, and they as well as the back leg are unfinished.
f) The signature is *Phiz, dl.*
g) The fork touches the plate near Mary, but the knife does not.

[PLATE B₂]

a) The fat boy's knife points upward.
b) Same as Plate B₁.
c) The chair back of Mary and farthest away is now shaded at the top.
d) Same as Plate B₁.
e) The braces of the fat boy's chair have now been outlined in black, and the fourth chair leg is better shown.
f) The signature is *Phiz, del.*
g) The knife touches the plate near Mary, but the fork does not.

A legend has been engraved on Plate B₂.

Part XIX · Plate 41 · Page 590

Mr. Weller and His Friends Drinking to Mr. Pell

The remarks given under the preceding plate apply also to this, which also, according to Hatton and Cleaver, was engraved in triplicate. Later the third plate received an engraved title. The design would have been much better had the ceiling heat domes been omitted, for they make the plate top-heavy. Plate A is much rarer than the other two.

[PLATE A]

a) A small bottle stands on the table near Mr. Pell's glass.
b) The floor boards run up and down.
c) There is a knife on the table between the bottle and the oyster shells.
d) There seem to be three or more horses racing in the picture on the wall.
e) The two buttons on the back of the coat of the coachman, whose back is prominent in the picture, has a design like the outline of a cat's face.
f) The second coachman from the right has a lock of hair showing behind his right eye.
g) The coachman at the right has two hardly distinguishable buttons on his coat near his left arm.

[P L A T E B₁]

a) There is no bottle on the table near Mr. Pell.

b) The floor boards run horizontally.

c) There is no knife to the left of the oyster shells, but there is one to the right.

d) There seem to be only two race horses.

e) The coachman's rear-buttons have designs which look like an S and an enantiomorphous S.

f) The second coachman from the right has no hair showing near his right eye.

g) The coachman at the right has four white buttons near his left arm.

[P L A T E B₂]

I think that this is a re-engraved and not a new plate.

a) As in Plate B₁.

b) As in Plate B₁.

c) As in Plate B₁.

d) As in Plate B₁.

e) The designs on the bottons look like V and τ.

f) The second coachman has a bit of hair near his right eye.

g) There are three white buttons and possibly a dark one below.

A legend has been engraved on Plate B₂.

Part XX · Plate 42 · Frontispiece

Parts XIX and XX of *Pickwick* came out together in November, 1837, as a single number. With it came Plates 40 and 41 and the Frontispiece and etched title. Two steels each were etched for the final two.

[P L A T E   A]

a) There are four stripes in Mr. Pickwick's footstool.
b) There is no paperknife between the inkstand and the book on the table.
c) The right cheek of the standing clown at the right is visible.
d) Sam Weller's right elbow rests on three books, which show dark edges.
e) The artist's signature, *Phiz, fecit,* is in the lower center, divided by a shield showing a sheep's-eyed Tupman portrait.
f) The cat is partly shaded.

[P L A T E   B]

a) There are six stripes on Mr. Pickwick's footstool.
b) There is a paperknife on the table.
c) The face of the standing clown at the right is turned more to his right than in Plate A.
d) The upper two of the books under Sam Weller's arm show white edges.
e) The artist's signature, *Phiz, del,* is at the left of the shield, upon which Mr. Tupman's eyes are not so much upturned as before.
f) The cat is white.

Plate B was used unchanged in the edition of 1838. No legend was added.

Part XX · Plate 43 · Etched Title

Two steels only were etched for the title page. There has been much discussion as to whether the Veller or the Weller plate was first. Since they were issued at the same time, however, neither can claim priority, although, of course, one was etched before the other.

[P L A T E   A]

a) The sign over the doorway of the inn reads *Tony Veller*, with several indecipherable lines.
b) The Marquis of Granby's arm in the sign is nearly fully extended, and he has no mustache.
c) The images at the sides of the doorway have their arms folded and end at the waist.
d) The signature is *PHIZ, fecit* at the lower center. ·

[P L A T E   B]

a) The sign reads *Tony Weller, licensed to sell beer, spirits, tobac.*
b) The Marquis' arm is bent at the elbow, and he has a mustache.
c) The images at the sides of the doorway being doubled up, now have only heads and legs.
d) The signature is *Phiz, fecᵗ.*

Plate B was used without change in the bound volume of 1838.

THE

PICKWICK PAPERS

BY

CHARLES DICKENS.

LONDON
CHAPMAN AND HALL 186 STRAND
MDCCCXXXVII.

THE

PICKWICK PAPERS

BY

CHARLES DICKENS.

LONDON
CHAPMAN AND HALL 186 STRAND
MDCCCXXXVII.

Plates 43A and 43B PICKWICK / 75

The
Life and Adventures
of

NICHOLAS NICKLEBY

The Life and Adventures of Nicholas Nickleby was begun in April, 1838, and continued until October, 1839. It appeared in twenty monthly parts, the nineteenth and twentieth together as one. Each part had two etchings by "Phiz," and, since the publishers expected as great a circulation as *The Pickwick Papers* had had, it was decided to etch each steel in duplicate, to avoid the confusion of having to make new plates later.

The number of copies sold of the first part showed a decided improvement over the anticipated number; consequently, beginning with Part II (or IV)[1], the number of steels for each plate, with the exception of numbers 7, 8, and 40, which remained in duplicate, was still further increased. According to Hatton and Cleaver (p. 134),[2] Plates 3, 4, 5, 6, 9, 10, 11, 12, 15, 16, 19, 20, 21, 22, 27, 28, 35, 36, 37, 38, and 39[3] were in triplicate, and Plates 13, 14, 17, 18, 23, 24, 25, 26, 29, 30, 31, 32, 33, and 34 in quad-

ruplicate. Since the designs were etched on quarto steel plates, each bearing two subjects, there were 64 quarto steels and 1 octavo for the 129 etchings, although Thomson, not counting the duplicate portraits of Plate 40, says there were 126 steels on 63 quarto plates; the miscount was due to the wrong number given for Plate 39. In enumerating the plates, minor variations, such as the presence or absence of the publishers' imprint at the bottom of Plates 1, 2, 3, 4, and 40, have not been taken into consideration in making up the total.

Since each plate and its mate or mates were printed simultaneously, then cut apart and bound up indiscriminately in the parts, one set is as much a first edition as another. It is, however, possible to determine in many cases the order in which the steels were etched, for some were numbered in either Arabic or Roman numerals.

The plates in *Nicholas Nickleby* differ from the early plates in *The Pickwick Papers* in having legends engraved below the designs. It has usually been stated that these legends were later

1. Whether triplicate plates began in Part II or Part IV depends upon whether Plates 3, 4, 5, and 6 were actually etched in triplicate.

2. Both Thomson (p. 110) and Hatton and Cleaver (p. 134) assert that there were three steels of Plates 3, 4, 5, and 6. In the following pages under these numbers, I show the third plates which I have and which appear to me to be more or less retouched but not duplicate plates.

3. Thomson (p. 110) erroneously says: "Plate 39 was drawn in duplicate on one plate and not repeated again." Hatton and Cleaver correctly state the number of steels as three, which may be seen from the reproductions given here under that plate number.

etched by "Phiz" upon the plates. However, since they were engraved and not etched, it is more than likely that this work was done by a professional engraver after the etchings were finished.

Browne's success with the *Pickwick* plates led to his employment by other writers, and in the nineteen months during which *Nickleby* ran he was busier than ever before. Between April, 1838, and October, 1839, he made a number of woodcuts and etched at least 91 plates besides the 129 for *Nickleby*. These were all of minor importance except the 22 etchings for Lever's *Harry Lorrequer*, which were drawn in Browne's most rollicking style, for Lever's stories appealed to his sense of humor. Most of these illustrations are exceptionally good, although there is a tendency toward overcrowding in some of the plates.

Part I · Plate 1 · Page 18

Mr. Ralph Nickleby's First Visit to His Poor Relations

Two steels were etched for this plate, and first impressions of each show the publishers' name and address, "London, Chapman & Hall, 186 Strand," below the legend. Both plates, however, are also found without this imprint. In the following pages the presence or absence of the publishers' name on Plates 1–4 inclusive is considered of no more importance than the retouching of a number of plates and neither has been counted in the enumeration of the steels. In etching this plate, "Phiz" began to use a roulette wheel to produce dots as halftone shading and continued doing so to the end.

Mr. Ralph Nickleby's first visit to his poor relations.

[PLATE A]

a) There is a vase on the mantel.
b) The doorknob at the right is dark.
c) The top edge of the door at the right is not shaded.
d) The door at the left has no knob.
e) The signature *PHIZ* is in capital letters.
f) The legend below the picture is 85 mm. long and in letters slightly larger than in the second plate.

Mr Ralph Nickleby's first visit to his poor relations.

[P L A T E   B]

a) There is nothing on the mantel.
b) The doorknob at the right is white.
c) The top edge of the door at the right is shaded by horizontal lines.
d) The door at the left has a knob.
e) The artist's signature is in backhand script.
f) The legend is 83.5 mm. long.

Part I · Plate 2 · Page 25

The Yorkshire Schoolmaster at "The Saracen's Head"

Like Plate 1, two steels were etched for this plate, and, like it, they are found with or without the publishers' imprint. Like so many other plates by "Phiz," the design is impaired by heavy shading at the top of the picture.

[P L A T E   A]

a) There are six cards stuck into the frame of the mirror over the mantel.
b) There is only one card adjacent to the larger, central one.
c) The cramps below the lamp shades extend over the edge of the glass.
d) The ring of the left bellpull is on a line with the extension of the top line of the mantel mirror.
e) There is a poster on the chimney breast at the right.
f) The title of the *Morning Herald* at the right is in two lines.
g) The artist's signature is in backhand capitals.

[P L A T E   B]

a) There are only four cards in the frame of the mantel mirror at the right.
b) There are two cards at the right of the large card on the mantel.
c) The cramps of the lamp shades do not extend over the bottom lines.
d) The ring of the left bellpull is below an extension of the top line of the mantel mirror.
e) There is no poster on the chimney breast.
f) The title of the newspaper is in one line.
g) The signature is in backhand script.

The Yorkshire Schoolmaster at "The Saracen's Head."

The Yorkshire Schoolmaster at The Saracen's Head.

Nicholas Starts for Yorkshire

Thomson, after listing the plates in *Nickleby* which were etched twice and those etched four times, said: "All the other subjects were etched three times"; and Hatton and Cleaver state that Plates 3, 4, 5, and 6 were etched three times. I have examined innumerable first editions of *Nickleby* and have as yet failed to find an undoubted third plate for Nos. 3, 4, 5, and 6. Even the third plate for No. 4, which shows more differences than the others, is such a faithful copy of the second that a close examination suggested only a rather extensive retouching of the preceding. Twelve enlarged photographs, made from these four doubtful plates, were sent to various bookdealers in this country and in London but failed to bring to light third plates showing greater differences than those in the four "B₂" plates reproduced here. I question the existence of third steels. However, for the record, I give reproductions of the four disputable plates.

[P L A T E   A]

a) The poster over Newman Noggs's hat is lettered in two lines, *Fast Trains. Reduced Fares,* and the poster to the right is marked *Spitfire.*
b) The brush near the two maids in the balcony shows its underside.
c) The hat of the boy at the left on top of the coach is dark.
d) Behind Newman Noggs there are only two men.
e) The top of the hat of the coachman flirting with the maids is white.
f) The flap on the pocket of the coachman reading the bill is not rectangular.
g) Mrs. Nickleby's hand does not show above Kate's head.
h) The signature *Phiz, del* is in script.
i) The legend measures 50.1 mm. from the dot at the bottom of the initial letter *N* to the period at the end. The publishers' imprint measures 32 mm.
j) The lid of the trunk near Squeers's feet has three nails on top.

Nicholas starts for Yorkshire.

Nicholas starts for Yorkshire.

Nicholas starts for Yorkshire.

a) The poster over Newman Noggs's hat is lettered only *Reduced Fares,* and the adjacent poster is not lettered at all.

b) The brush near the maids does not show the underside.

c) The hat of the boy at the left on the coach is light.

d) Behind Newman there are three men, one of whom holds a pitchfork.

e) The top of the hat of the flirtatious coachman is dark.

f) The pocket flap of the man reading the bill is approximately rectangular. The rim of his glasses is a solid black line.

g) Mrs. Nickleby's hand shows above Kate's head.

h) The signature is reversed.

i) The legend measures 50.0 mm., and the publishers' imprint 30.8 mm.

j) The trunk near Squeers's feet has five nails in the top of the lid.

[PLATE B₂]

The legend on this plate measures 53 mm., and the publishers' imprint 39.0 mm. The left rim of the glasses of the man reading the bill is a double line, and there are only four nailheads showing on the upper side of the lid of the trunk beside Squeers. There are also many slight changes in the shading, which, however, look to me like retouching. The plate itself is such a close copy of Plate B₁ that it appears to me questionable whether it is a new plate or Plate B₁ retouched. The fact that the legends and publishers' imprint are of different lengths might possibly be accounted for by the fact that it was easier to engrave a new one than it was to patch up an old one that was worn out.

Part II · Plate 4 · Page 45

The Five Sisters of York

This plate, as mentioned under Plate 3, is said to have been etched in triplicate, but the third plate so meticulously follows the lines of the second, even to the lines of shading, that it appears more probable that the third plate represents a retouching of the second, in spite of the different lengths of the engraved legends of the two.

The Five Sisters of York.

[PLATE A]

a) The signature *PHIZ* in capitals is almost lost in the shading of the large rock in the right foreground.

b) There are two small birds in the sky at the right of the church steeple.

c) There is but one swan on the river.

d) The upright of the crucifix in the priest's hand is white.

e) The thread held by both the second and the third girl is broken, and one strand touches the other at the left of the break.

f) The cap of the first girl at the left has no dots between the crossed lines, and the design on her taboret shows diagonal crossed lines.

g) There are no dots around the edges of the purse of the second girl, and no buttons show on her coat.

h) Only three fingers show above the middle joints of the right hand of the third girl, although there are four toward the tips. The little finger is not tightly closed.

i) The fourth girl has only a single row of dark dots on the front of her coat.

j) There is a design on the back of the taboret of the fifth girl.

k) The shape of the rock in the foreground differs from that in the other plates in having a much sharper point.

l) The length of the legend from the dot at the bottom of the initial T to the period at the end is **44.5 mm**.

The Five Sisters of York.

[P L A T E B₁]

a) The signature is in script and is reversed.

b) There is one large bird at the left of the steeple.

c) There are two swans in the river and a child (?) on the bank.

d) The crucifix is dark.

e) The threads between the second and third girl do not cross.

f) There are dots on the cap of the girl at the left. Her taboret does not show diagonal lines.

g) The second girl's purse has dots around the border, and there are two rows of buttons on her coat.

h) Four of the fingers of the third girl's right hand show above the middle joint, and three are nearly closed. There is no ring on her third finger. The double vertical lines of the pattern of her skirt, second to the left of her purse, end at the lower horizontal stripe.

i) The fourth girl has a double row of dots on the front of her coat.

j) There is no design on the back of the taboret of the fifth girl.

k) The rock in the foreground is not so pointed as before.

l) The legend measures 51.3 mm., and the publishers' imprint measures 37.8 mm.

a–b) Same as in Plate B₁.

c) There are two swans in the river and a goat (?) on the shore line.

d) Same as in Plate B₁.

e) The threads between the second and third girl cross.

f–g) Same as in Plate B₁.

h) Four of the fingers of the third girl's right hand show above the middle joint, and three are nearly closed, as in Plate B₁. There is a ring on her third finger. The vertical lines of the pattern on her skirt at the left of her purse extend nearly as far upward as the top of her purse.

i–k) Same as in Plate B₁.

l) The engraved legend from the dot in the initial *T* to the period at the end measures 46.6 mm., and the publishers' imprint measures 30 mm.

The third girl's eyelids in Plate B₂ do not show the upper lines as they do in Plate B₁, and the crossed lines of the first girl's cap curve differently, but these slight differences, as well as the differences in the lengths of the legends, may easily be accounted for by retouching.

The Five Sisters of York

Part III · Plate 5 · Page 68

The Internal Economy of Dotheboys Hall

This plate is said to have been etched in triplicate, but see the note under Plate 3. My own opinion is that there were but two steels. Beginning here, the publishers no longer added their imprint at the bottom of the page.

a) The plate is not signed.

b) The rafters do not show above the door.

c) Squeers's stick points to the left of Nicholas' shoulder.

d) There are no buttons on Mrs. Squeers's coat.

e) The hand of the fifth boy from the left and at the back does not show, and the eyes of the second boy at Mrs. Squeers's right are downcast.

f) The legend measures 68.0 mm.

[P L A T E   B₁]

a) The signature of *Phiz* is in very small script.

b) The rafters above the door are only roughly sketched in.

c) Squeers's stick crosses Nicholas' vest and touches his shirt front.

d) Several buttons show on Mrs. Squeers's coat.

e) The hand of the fifth boy standing at the left shows, and the eyes of the second boy at Mrs. Squeers's right are turned toward her.

f) The legend measures 68.5 mm. from the dot in the initial letter to the period at the end.

[P L A T E   B₂]

There are differences in the shading in various parts of this design, but, except for these slight changes, it seems to be Plate B₁. The legend is 68.5 mm. long, as before.

The internal economy of Dotheboys Hall.

The internal economy of Dotheboys Hall

The internal economy of Dotheboys Hall

Part III · Plate 6 · Page 89

Kate Nickleby Sitting to Miss La Creevy

This plate is said to have been etched in triplicate, but see the note under Plate 3. Much about Plate B₂ suggests that it is new.

Kate Nickleby sitting to Miss La Creevy

[P L A T E   A]

a) All of Ralph Nickleby's hat and foot shows.
b) The large picture above the mantel has the figures *2* and *3* on the vertical sides of the frame. Between it and the two to the left, there is a small oval picture. The medium-sized one still farther to the left has nothing above it but the suspension cords.
c) To the right of the mantel the lower one of the four frames in a vertical row is oval.
d) The picture Miss La Creevy is painting looks like a three-quarter-length portrait.
e) Kate has a couple of small flowers in her hand.
f) The screen back of Kate is very sketchily decorated.
g) Miss La Creevy's stool is not heavily shaded.
h) The legs of the chair back of her are apparently square.
i) There is a picture on the wall back of the sketching cupid.
j) The legend is 67.0 mm. long.
k) The smaller cat in the foreground is more white than black.

[P L A T E   B₁]

a) About three-fourths of Ralph Nickleby's hat and half of his foot show.
b) The large picture over the mantel has no numbers on the sides. Left of it there are two square pictures, then farther left a moderately large one with a small oval frame above it.
c) To the right of the mantel in the vertical row of four pictures, the lowest one is square.
d) The picture that Miss La Creevy is painting looks more like a house than a portrait.
e) Kate has something in her hand that looks like a bunch of earthworms.
f) The screen back of Kate has quite an elaborate design on it.

g) Miss La Creevy's stool is shaded so that it is quite dark.
h) The legs of the chair back of Miss La Creevy seem to be turned.
i) There is no picture on the wall back of the cupid.
j) The legend is 66.5 mm. long.
k) The small cat is darker than in Plate A, and the tail of the large one touches its paw.

Kate Nickleby sitting to Miss La Creevy.

Kate Nickleby sitting to Miss La Creevy.

[P L A T E B₂]

While this plate is a very close copy of the preceding one, it shows so many changes in the shade lines that it was either very extensively retouched or actually from a new steel. In most cases the changes are difficult to describe in words. The legend is ½ mm. shorter than the preceding one, and there is also a difference in the heights of the capital letters. The loop of the *K* in Plate B₁ is tangent to the letter *t* extended, while in Plate B₂ it does not go so far to the right. The *N* of Plate B₁ does not extend so far upward, and there

are other slight differences. If the old plate was extensively worn, the legend may have been burnished out and re-engraved. Other changes are: a white space in Plate B₂ between the tail of the large cat and the paw of the smaller one and slight differences in the writing on the portfolio below the foot of Kate's chair, the shading on the top of the raised platform upon which the chair stands, and the pictures on the wall.

If it were not for the fact that the other third plates that accompanied Parts II and III were only very doubtfully new, I might be inclined to think this one actually new.

Newman Noggs Leaves the Ladies in the Empty House

Plate 7 was etched in duplicate.

[PLATE A]

Newman Noggs leaves the ladies in the empty house.

a) There are no vertical lines, as of a door or window casing, back of Newman Noggs.
b) The upper left windowpane is not cracked, and the chimney stack showing through the right panes is blunt.
c) There is no spiderweb over the door.
d) The middle rail of the chair back of Mrs. Nickleby is not bifurcated at the top, and the upper part is not entirely shaded.
e) Mrs. Nickleby's two hands do not touch.
f) The chair back of Kate has only three spokes.
g) Ties show on Noggs's shoes.
h) There is a mouse on the floor in the foreground.
i) The teakettle is shown completely.
j) The fender is almost straight along the top edge.
k) The legend from the dot in the initial letter to the period is 84.5 mm. long.

[PLATE B]

a) There are three vertical lines back of Newman Noggs.
b) The upper left windowpane is cracked, and the chimney stack showing through the window is tall and tapering.
c) There is a spiderweb over the door.
d) The middle rail of the chair back of Mrs. Nickleby is divided at the top, and it is entirely dark.
e) Mrs. Nickleby's hands touch.
f) The chair back of Kate has five spokes.
g) There are no ties on Noggs's shoes.
h) The mouse has become a rat.
i) The teakettle handle is incomplete at the left.
j) The fender shows a curved upper edge.
k) The legend is 79.0 mm. long.

Newman Noggs leaves the ladies in the empty house.

Nicholas Astonishes Mr. Squeers and Family

This plate was etched in duplicate. For a mob scene the drawing is good, but if the sketchy ceiling beams had been omitted, it would have been better. Mrs. Squeers is rather too dilapidated looking and Miss Squeers too old.

[P L A T E   A]

a) At the upper right the topmost boy stands alone.
b) The handle of Miss Squeers's push-broom is mostly dark.
c) The inkwell in the center above the crowd is not clearly drawn, there is no inkwell in the air at the far left, and there are three inkwells on the floor.
d) The right sleeve of the boy just to the left of the central flying inkwell is dark.
e) An arm of one of the boys extends to the left beyond the remainder of the design.
f) The ribbon of Mrs. Squeers's bonnet is not shown.
g) Nicholas' stick is mostly dark.

[P L A T E   B]

a) There are two boys at the upper right instead of one.
b) The handle of Miss Squeers's broom is light.
c) The inkwell above the center of the crowd is clearly defined, and there is another in the air to the left. There are but two on the floor.
d) The right arm of the boy between the two flying inkwells is not heavily shaded.
e) There is no boy's arm extending to the left beyond the rest of the design.
f) A ribbon from Mrs. Squeers's bonnet is shown extending to the extreme left of the picture.
g) Nicholas' stick is shown by parallel lines.

Nicholas astonishes Mr Squeers and family.

Nicholas astonishes Mr Squeers and family.

Part V · Plate 9 · Page 153

Nicholas Engaged as Tutor in a Private Family

There were three steels made for Plate 9 because the phenomenal sales of the monthly parts of *Nickleby* required the printing of the three to keep up with the printing of the text.

[PLATE A]

a) There are two pictures on the wall to the left of the mirror.
b) There is only a candle on the mantel.
c) The glass on the table at the right has no spoon in it.
d) Miss Petowker has on a plaid dress with both vertical and horizontal stripes defined by several lines. She also wears a string of beads and has a band, which appears convex upward, above her forehead.
e) Mrs. Kenwigs' right thumb shows.
f) Nicholas' chair back has vertical shading.
g) The poker lies near the front edge of the fender.
h) The artist's signature is in script, followed by a word which may be intended for "fecit."

[PLATE B]

a) There is only one picture to the left of the mirror.
b) There are a candle and a jar on the mantel.
c) There is a spoon in the tumbler on the table.
d) Miss Petowker's dress is plaid, but the horizontal stripes are shown by single lines. She wears no beads, and the band across her hair is straight.
e) Mrs. Kenwigs' right thumb does not show.
f) Nicholas' chair back is white, with just a fancy scroll made by single lines.
g) The poker lies at the back of the fender.
h) The artist's signature at the lower right is a very faint *Phiz, del,* in script.

Nicholas engaged as Tutor in a private family.

Nicholas engaged as Tutor in a private family.

Nicholas engaged as Tutor in a private family.

94 / NICKLEBY *Plates 9B and 9C*

a–c) As in Plate B.

d) Miss Petowker's dress has vertical stripes and is dark. There are no beads and no band across her hair.

e) As in Plate B.

f) The back of Nicholas' chair is lightly shaded.

g) As in Plate B.

h) The signature is *PHIZ* in small capitals at the lower right. There is another signature, partly effaced by the floor shading, just below the rear leg of the baby's chair.

Part V · Plate 10 · Page 157

Miss Mantalini Introduces Kate to Miss Knag

[P L A T E   A]

a) The girl's hat on the shelf is seen from the underside. There is nothing on the shelf below.

b) The girl in the lower right corner has on a plain dress, and the girl back of her has on a white apron.

c) The girl at the extreme left has a band around her hair, and the one standing in front of her has a plain dress and a bandeau.

d) The bandeau of the girl back of Kate extends across her hair. Only her left hand shows.

e) The hamper has lines crossed at right angles on the side and inside the lid, and there is a cloth on the floor nearby.

f) The artist's signature *PHIZ* in the lower right corner is in capital letters.

Madame Mantalini introduces Kate to Miss Knag.

[P L A T E   B]

a) The hat on the shelf is a poke bonnet. There is a jar on the shelf below.

b) The girl in the lower right corner has on a plaid dress, and the girl back of her has no apron.

c) The girl at the extreme left wears no bandeau, nor does the girl standing in front of her. The latter's dress is flowered.

d) The bandeau of the girl back of Kate ends in front of her ear. Her two hands show but are hazy.

e) The hamper is basket-woven, and there is no cloth on the floor nearby.

f) The artist's signature is a small and cramped script *Phiz, del.*

[P L A T E   C]

a) Same as in Plate B.

b) The plaid dress is more marked. The girl at the back has no apron.

c) The girl at the left, as in Plate B, has no bandeau, but she is better looking. The girl in front of her is as in Plate B.

d) The bandeau of the girl back of Kate ends above her ear.

e) Same as in Plate B.

f) The signature *Phiz, del* is in script.

Madame Mantalini introduces Kate to Miss Knag.

Madame Mantalini introduces Kate to Miss Knag.

Part VI · Plate 11 · Page 175

Miss Nickleby Introduced to Her Uncle's Friends

This plate was etched in triplicate. Two of the plates bear numbers indicating the order of engraving.

[P L A T E   A]

a) The plate is not numbered.
b) The artist's signature "*PHIZ*" is in small capitals nearly in the center below.
c) There is no house in the large picture on the wall.
d) The trousers of the man seated at the left are dark, the edge of his chair is shaded, and there are fringes near his shoulder.
e) The statuette on the mantel stands up straight.
f) The clock shows five o'clock.
g) Ralph Nickleby's right hand is back up.
h) The footman has epaulets.

[P L A T E   B]

a) There is a small number *2* in the lower right corner. If it were not for that, I should have put the next plate (C) second, for in some ways it more closely resembles Plate A.
b) The signature *PHIZ* is left of the lower center, larger than in Plate A.
c) There is the gable end of a house in the picture on the wall.
d) The trousers of the man at the left are light, the edge of his chair is light, and there are no fringes near the top.
e) The statuette on the mantel looks as though it had eaten green apples.
f) The clock shows a few minutes after ten o'clock.
g) Ralph Nickleby's right hand is palm up.
h) There are no epaulets on the footman's shoulder.

Miss Nickleby introduced to her Uncle's friends

Miss Nickleby introduced to her Uncle's friends.

Miss Nickleby introduced to her Uncle's friends

a) The plate is numbered *3* in the lower right corner.

b) The signature *PHIZ* extends into the shading of the foreground.

c) The picture on the wall shows the gable end of a house and a man or woman in front.

d) The trousers of the man at the left are shaded, the edge of his chair is slightly shaded, and there are no fringes.

e) The statuette stands upright.

f) The clock indicates five o'clock.

g) Ralph Nickleby's hands are about as in Plate B.

h) There is a suggestion of epaulets on the footman's shoulder.

Mr. Ralph Nickleby's Honest Composure

This plate was engraved in triplicate. Plates 2 and 3 are clearly numbered, and possibly a short vertical line after the signature of the other is intended for a figure 1.

[P L A T E   A]

a) The signature, in italic capitals, is near the lower center, and after it are two vertical scratches, one of which doubtfully may represent the numeral 1.
b) The middle bookshelf shows the left-hand books lying on their sides and the adjacent two standing straight up. The lower shelf shows no book lying on its side.
c) Through the open door, the casing of another door or window shows.
d) Nicholas' left hand forms a fist on his chest.
e) There is a suggestion of braces between the legs of the chair.

[P L A T E   B]

a) This plate is numbered *2* in the paraph after the signature *PHIZ* and also at the lower left.
b) The second bookshelf shows the right-end book lying at an angle, and the lower shelf shows the ends of two books at the right lying flat.
c) The open door shows no other door casing.
d) Nicholas' left hand shows the index finger pointing to his right side.
e) The chair shows one distinct brace.

[P L A T E   C]

a) There is a figure *3* at the lower right edge of the floor boards. The signature *Phiz* has a small *o* after it.
b) The second bookshelf is much like that in Plate A except that both books have raised bands on their backs. The lower shelf shows fewer books.
c) The open door shows a door casing beyond.
d) Nicholas' hand is as in Plate B.
e) The chair shows no trace of a brace between the legs.

Mr. Ralph Nickleby's honest composure.

Mr Ralph Nickleby's 'honest' composure.

Mr Ralph Nickleby's 'honest' composure.

Part VII · Plate 13 · Page 196

The Professional Gentlemen at Madame Mantalini's

There were four steels of Plate 13, the increasing number suggesting the increasing popularity of *Nickleby*. All the plates are marked with numbers, which may indicate the actual order of engraving and probably does. It has been suggested that the numbers were etched on the plates later, but it is absurd to suppose that the plates were waxed, etched, and immersed again in acid just for the numbers. They may have been engraved, but it is doubtful, for they are not neat enough for the work of anyone familiar with engraving tools.

The drawing for this plate is rather fantastic, although I suppose the weird creations called women's hats and bonnets are no more peculiar than those of the present day.

[P L A T E   A]

a) This plate is marked with the figure *1* below the dressmaker's dummy at the right.
b) The ballet dancer in the picture on the left wall has her legs crossed, and her right hand is apparently holding up her skirt.
c) Mr. Mantalini's right hand shows four fingers, the index finger well bent, the other three slightly so.
d) The hat on the right of the mirror shows a flower under the brim, with a squirmy line below it. The hat between Kate and the man with the stick is sketched with very little detail.
e) The hat and stick of the fat "gentleman" are reflected in the mirror.
f) The door behind the mirror shows three panels at the left.
g) The artist's signature is in italic capitals in the lower center. No flourishes precede or follow it.

[P L A T E   B]

a) This plate is clearly marked with a *2* below the dummy.
b) In the picture on the left wall, the ballet dancer's legs are not crossed, and her right hand is near her head.
c) Mr. Mantalini's right hand shows his index and little fingers extended upward.
d) The hat on the right of the mirror shows no flower under the brim.
e) The reflection in the mirror is similar to that in Plate A, although more of the hat shows.
f) The door behind the mirror shows only a single panel at the left.
g) The artist's signature is *PHIZ* in italic capitals, with dots before and after it. There are no flourishes.

[P L A T E   C]

a) A curlicue at the lower left looks like the figure *3* and was probably so intended. There is another at the lower right.
b) The picture on the left wall shows the dancer with both arms raised and legs crossed.
c) Mr. Mantalini's fingers are as in Plate B but shorter.
d) The hat on the mirror shows an ornament that looks like the figure *3* with a *10* below it. There is no hat behind Kate's shoulder.
e) There is no reflection in the mirror.
f) The door behind the mirror shows two panels at the left.
g) The artist's signature is in the lower center and is in italic capitals with curlicues before and after.

[P L A T E   D]

a) At the lower left there is a figure *4* lying sidewise, and this seems to be the plate number, although there is also a curlicue at the lower right which looks like a number *3*.
b) The picture on the left shows the dancer's two arms raised, and the complete line of the bottom of her skirt shows as an oval.
c) Mr. Mantalini's right hand shows three fingers raised and the index finger bent so that it nearly touches his thumb.
d) The hat on the mirror shows a three-petal rose. The hat behind Kate is shown in simple outline.
e) The reflection in the mirror is almost the same as in Plate A.
f) The door behind the mirror shows three panels at the left.
g) The artist's signature is somewhat to the right of the lower center and looks like "PHIS" with a dot before and after it.

The Professional Gentlemen at Madame Mantalini's.

The Professional Gentlemen at Madame Mantalini's.

The Professional Gentlemen at Madame Mantalinis

The Professional Gentlemen at Madame Mantalinis.

Part VII · Plate 14 · Page 209

The Country Manager Rehearses a Combat

This illustration was etched four times, with two subjects on each quarto plate. They are easily distinguished, for three are marked below the chair at the right with the numerals *1*, *2*, and *3*, and in the same place on the fourth plate there are some scratches which may be intended for a 4. In all the plates the landlady stands in the doorway, although the text calls for the landlord.

[PLATE A]

a) The plate is marked *1* below the nearest leg of the chair at the right.
b) The pistol on the floor touches the knee of the "big 'un."
c) The signature *PHIZ* is at the lower right corner.
d) The lower end of the newel post and the steps are not clearly shown.
e) The man on the horse in the picture over the door has a whip, the man behind him has none.
f) There is a triangular "spitbox" below Crummles' right foot, though it is nearly lost in the shading of the floor.
g) There are many minor changes in details of shading in the four plates, but the number on the plate is sufficient to identify it.

[PLATE B]

a) The plate has the number *2* below the chair at the right.
b) The pistol does not touch the large sailor's knee.
c) The signature *PHIZ* is in the lower center.
d) The lower end of the newel post is clearly shown, and the floor boards below it run up and down, while in the other three plates they are not shown.
e) The man on the horse in the picture has only a stub of a whip, the man behind has none.
f) There is no cuspidor.

[PLATE C]

a) The plate is marked *3* below the chair.
b) The pistol does not touch the sailor's knee.
c) The signature of the artist is to the right of the center.
d) The lower end of the newel post is shown, and six steps are clearly seen. No boards are shown below.
e) The man on the horse in the picture and the man behind him have whips.
f) There is no cuspidor.

[PLATE D]

a) The plate is marked with some scratches which are apparently intended for the figure **4**.
b) The pistol does not touch the knee of the sailor.
c) The artist's signature is in the lower right corner and looks like "PHI" followed by one small *s* over another.
d) The lower end of the newel post shows, stair steps are indefinite, and there are no floor boards.
e) The man on the horse in the picture has a whip, the other man has none.
f) There is no cuspidor.

The Country Manager rehearses a Combat.

The Country Manager rehearses a Combat.

The Country Manager rehearses a Combat

The Country Manager rehearses a Combat.

The Great Bespeak for Miss Snevellicci

Of this subject there were three etchings, marked *1, 2,* or *3* in the lower right corners. All are signed *PHIZ*, with the *Z* reversed.

[P L A T E   A]

a) The plate is numbered *1* at the lower right, behind the wing.
b) The footlights are all perfect and vertical.
c) The fruit falling from the basket of the orange vendor shows one orange on the first board, two on the second, and one on the third.
d) The young officer has a standing lock of hair, a monocle in his right eye, and a sword near his cane.
e) There is a program hanging over the rail of the upper balcony.

[P L A T E   B]

a) The plate is marked *2* at the lower right.
b) The fifth footlight from the right is inclined, and the sixth has a broken glass.
c) The fruit shows one in the air, one on the first board, and two on the next.
d) The young officer's hair is smoothed down but is light, for he is evidently a blond. He has neither monocle nor sword.
e) Same as in Plate A.

[P L A T E   C]

a) The plate is marked *3.*
b) The fifth and sixth footlights from the left are inclined toward each other.
c) The fruit shows two on the first board, two on the second, and one on the third.
d) The officer's hair is the same as in Plate B, except that it is darker.
e) There is no program hanging over the balcony.

The great bespeak for Miss Snevellicci

The great bespeak for Miss Snevellicci

The great bespeak for Miss Snevellicci

Nicholas Instructs Smike in the Art of Acting

This plate was etched in triplicate and numbered, respectively, *1*, *2*, and *3* at the lower right near the legs of the chair. In Plate 3, the word "in" was omitted from the off-center legend.

[P L A T E   A]

a) The number *1* appears at the right of the back leg of the chair.
b) The signature at the bottom center is in capital letters with a dot before and a dot after it.
c) There is no mug on the table.
d) The back of the chair shows a pattern.
e) The wing or screen back of Smike shows two crossbars.
f) There is a hat on the floor in the foreground.
g) A brace is faintly shown on the dark wing at the right.
h) There is no candle in the bottle on the table.
i) The front strap holding Nicholas' sword is white at the upper end.

[P L A T E   B]

a) The number *2* appears at the lower right between the front and rear legs of the chair.
b) The signature is in the center and resembles that in Plate A.
c) There is no mug on the table.
d) Similar to Plate A.
e) Only one crossbar appears in the screen.
f) Same as in Plate A.
g) There is no brace on the dark wing.
h) There is no candle in the bottle.
i) The entire strap is white.

[P L A T E   C]

a) The plate is numbered *3* in the same position as in Plate B.
b) The signature is at the center within the shading of the floor.
c) There is a mug on the table back of the spear.

Nicholas instructs Smike in the Art of Acting.

d) The shading of the wing has been carried through the chair back.
e) There is only one brace, as in Plate B.
f) In the place of the hat on the floor, there are now a dagger, a shield, and a goblet(?).
g) The brace is clearly defined.
h) There is a candle in the bottle.
i) The entire strap is dark.

Nicholas instructs Smike the Art of Acting.

Nicholas instructs Smike in the Art of Acting.

Affectionate Behavior of Messrs Pyke and Pluck

This plate was etched in quadruplicate, but only the fourth one is definitely marked with a number.

[P L A T E   A]

a) There are four shelves hanging on the wall.
b) The signature *PHIZ* is in italic capitals, preceded and followed by flourishes. It is possible that a slanting line within the end loop is intended for the figure 1.
c) The upper corner of Mr. Pyke's chair is blank.
d) There is a poker in the fender.
e) Three fingers of Mr. Pluck's left hand turn inward, so that the tips do not show.
f) The cat's tail is not clearly shown, and she has a dark ribbon around her neck.

[P L A T E   B]

a) Same as in Plate A.
b) The signature is in sloping capitals; the final *Z* looks like the figure *2*.
c) There are three vertical strokes in the upper corner of the chair.
d) Same as in Plate A but more lightly etched.
e) Pluck's little finger shows.
f) The end of the cat's tail and the ribbon are white.

[P L A T E   C]

a) There are only three shelves.
b) The signature is partly within the dots of the floor shading. No number found.
c) There are five horizontal lines in the corner block of the chair.
d) There is no poker.
e) Nearly the same as in Plate B, but the little finger is bent less.
f) The cat's tail and ribbon are as in Plate B.

Affectionate behaviour of Mess.ᵈˢ Pyke & Pluck.

Affectionate behaviour of Mess.rs Pyke & Pluck.

Affectionate behaviour of Mess.rs Pyke & Pluck.

Affectionate behaviour of Messrs Pyke & Pluck.

a) There are four shelves.
b) There is no signature. A figure *4* appears at the lower left.
c) There is one vertical line in the corner block of the chair.
d) The poker is much as in Plates A and B.
e) Pluck's fist is closed, and the fingers turn up, so that part of the index finger shows.
f) The cat's tail and ribbon are similar to those in Plate C, but the cat shows more white on its hip.

Part IX · Plate 18 · Page 288

Nicholas Hints at the Probability of His Leaving the Company

Etched in quadruplicate, the third and fourth plates have marks that appear to be numbers, the others are not numbered. The expressions on the faces of the actors on hearing the news that Nicholas may leave the company are excellent: the men glad to have him go, the women disappointed.

[PLATE A]

a) The signature *PHIZ* is engraved backwards, and there is a dot preceding the reversed *Z*.
b) There is no trident in the foreground.
c) The tall man with the Scotch cap has a mustache and some whiskers under his chin. The feather in his cap has two small ones at its base.
d) The fat man with three feathers in his cap has a one-sided smile.
e) The skirt of the girl at the extreme right is not shaded over her hip. The border is shown by closely spaced vertical lines.
f) Nicholas has no cane.

[P L A T E   B]

a) The signature has the *Z* reversed, and there is one dot before and one after the name.
b) There is a trident on the floor behind the "savage."
c) The tall man has no mustache but a bit of whisker on his chin. The feathers are as in Plate A.
d) The fat man's mouth is puckered as though he is saying "prunes."
e) The girl's skirt is completely shaded with up-and-down lines, and the border is accentuated by short lines and a broken line above.
f) Nicholas has a cane.

[P L A T E   C]

a) The signature of *Phiz* is in capital letters, inclined, and with curlicues before and after, the former with a dot, the latter with a line which resembles a figure 3.
b) There is a trident on the floor.
c) The tall man has a mustache and galways, but there are no small feathers at the base of the tall one.
d) The fat man's mouth is open.
e) The girl's skirt has a border defined by a line and several dots.
f) Nicholas has a cane.

[P L A T E   D]

a) There is no signature. There is a figure *4* at the lower right.
b) There is a trident on the floor.
c) The tall man has no mustache but has a bit of a beard.
d) The fat man's mouth is slightly open.
e) The girl's skirt has a border defined by a line and vertical shading.
f) Nicholas has a cane.

Nicholas hints at the probability of his leaving the Company

Nicholas hints at the probability of his leaving the Company.

Nicholas hints at the probability of his leaving the Company.

Nicholas hints at the probability of his leaving the Company.

Theatrical Emotion of Mr. Vincent Crummles

This plate was etched in triplicate, each plate numbered in Arabic numerals at the lower right.

[PLATE A]

a) The plate has the number *1* above the foot of the boy at the right.
b) The signature is in backhand script, preceded and followed by wavy lines in the lower center.
c) One of the two men at the left has his arm across the other's shoulder.
d) The poster at the left shows a very sketchy stagecoach headed left. Beneath this are the words *Railroad Speed* and some horizontal lines.
e) The word *Ports* . . . appears on the door of the coach.
f) There is a cloth without dots in Crummles' hand.
g) The right side of the lantern over the door shows only up-and-down lines.

[PLATE B]

a) The number *2* appears below and to the left of the foot of the boy at the right.
b) The signature in capitals is preceded and followed by wavy lines.
c) The man who was at the extreme left has moved forward so that his face shows in front of his companion. He now wears a hat.
d) The poster overhead now bears almost indecipherable words, *Reduc* . . . and *Port*. . . .
e) There is no name on the door of the coach.
f) None of the cloth, which now bears dots, appears to the left of Crummles' hand.
g) The right side of the lantern now has both horizontal and vertical shade lines.

Theatrical emotion of Mr Vincent Crummles.

Theatrical emotion of Mr Vincent Crummles.

Theatrical emotion of Mᵣ Vincent Crummles.

a) The number *3* is farther to the left than the number in Plate B.
b) The signature *Phiz* in backhand script is followed by a wavy line.
c) The man who was moved forward in Plate B now wears no hat.
d) The poster overhead shows a coach driving to the right, below which are the words *Railroad Speed. . . . Toda . . . Winches. . . .*
e) There is an undecipherable name on the coach door.
f) The dotted cloth in Crummles' hand shows partly at the left of it.
g) The right side of the lantern shows fewer horizontal lines than in Plate B.

Part X · Plate 20 · Page 310

Nicholas Attracted by the Mention of His Sister's Name in the Coffee Room

This plate was etched in triplicate, each plate numbered at the lower right in Arabic numerals.

[P L A T E   A]

a) There is a number *1* below the table at the right.
b) The signature in backhand script is preceded and followed by wavy lines.
c) The support of the chandelier is shown by two lines ending at the lower end in a small ball, which is disconnected from the lamp itself.
d) There is a wineglass on the table of the man behind Nicholas.
e) The list on the mantel is clearly marked *WINE*.
f) The boat below the foliage in the picture on the wall at the left is headed to the left, but it is very sketchily drawn.
g) There is no masthead to the paper in Nicholas' hand.
h) The stock of the man behind Nicholas shows no bowknot.

a) This plate is numbered *2* below the table at the right.

b) The signature is followed and preceded by wavy lines; the one at the right shows, within the loop, a curve and straight line which might be interpreted as another *2*.

c) The support of the chandelier is shown by three parallel lines which are rather ragged.

d) There is no wineglass on the table of the man behind Nicholas.

e) The list on the mantel shows the letters *WI*.

f) The boat seems to have a sail.

g) The masthead of Nicholas' newspaper is indicated by vertical lines.

h) The man behind Nicholas has no bowknot on his stock, but it has more shadow below it than in Plate A.

[P L A T E   C]

a) This plate is numbered *3* below the table at the right.

b) The signature is cursive but not preceded by a curlicue, though followed by one which begins with a clear figure *3*.

c) The chandelier support is shown by several parallel lines.

d) There is a wineglass on the table behind Nicholas.

e) The list on the mantel shows only a letter *W* followed by three short lines.

f) The boat is headed left and is better drawn than in Plate A or Plate B.

g) The masthead of Nicholas' paper is indicated by a horizontal line.

h) The man's stock shows a bowknot as a tie.

Nicholas attracted by the mention of his Sister's name in the Coffee Room.

Nicholas attracted by the mention of his Sister's name in the Coffee Room.

Nicholas attracted by the mention of his Sister's name in the Coffee Room.

Mr. and Mrs. Mantalini in Ralph Nickleby's Office

This plate was etched three times, each plate numbered in the lower corner of the map on the wall behind Ralph Nickleby's chair. The picture, in general, is very good, except that Mr. Mantalini is too much of a caricature. If "Phiz" had given both Mr. and Mrs. Mantalini more forehead, it would have been better. However, that is a fault not uncommon to artists of the period, as, for example, Cruikshank's picture in *Oliver Twist* of Fagin in the condemned cell.

[P L A T E   A]

a) The number *1* is rather faint in the corner of the map.
b) The signature *PHIZ* is preceded and followed by curlicues.
c) There is no almanac on the wall.
d) There is no crack in the windowpane.
e) Mantalini has only one ring on his right hand.
f) Only the thumb of the glove on the floor touches the cane.
g) There is only one lock on each of the deedboxes on the high shelf.
h) The long top drawer of the desk below the ledger shows no knob.

[P L A T E   B]

a) The figure *2* on the map is very clear.
b) The signature in italic capitals has an ornamental *P* and a dot between the *I* and the *Z*.
c) There is an almanac on the wall between Mr. and Mrs. Mantalini.
d) The windowpane is cracked.
e) Mantalini wears three rings.
f) The thumb and middle finger of the glove touch the cane.
g) The deedbox at the left has three locks, the one at the right, one.
h) The long top drawer of the desk has no knob.

Mr. and Mrs. Mantalini in Ralph Nickleby's Office.

Mr and Mrs Mantalini in Ralph Nicklebys Office.

Mr and Mrs Mantalini in Ralph Nicklebys Office.

[P L A T E C]

a) The figure *3* is partly obliterated by shade lines and is imperfect.

b) The signature *PHIZ* is without ornamentation.

c) There is no almanac on the wall.

d) Same as in Plate B.

e) Mantalini wears two rings, one rather broad; perhaps also one on his forefinger.

f) The thumb of the glove almost touches the cane, the index finger crosses it.

g) The left deedbox has three locks, the right one shows only a keyhole.

h) The long top drawer of the desk shows a knob in front of Mrs. Mantalini's extended right hand.

Part XI · Plate 22 · Page 351

Emotion of Mr. Kenwigs on Hearing the Family News from Nicholas

This plate was etched in triplicate. While this drawing cannot be considered beautiful artistically, it is very successful as an illustration showing the confusion existing in the house of Kenwigs.

[PLATE A]

a) There is a very faint number *1* below the floor shading in the lower right corner. There is only one dot in the artist's signature.

b) The signature is in italic capitals with a little open-center dot after it.

c) The child's bonnet at the right end of the clotheslines is without tie strings.

d) The lower of the two pictures at the right of the mirror shows a girl with both arms down.

e) There is no man in the archway of the castle on the mantel.

f) There is nothing falling from the spoon in the hands of the nurse.

g) The cup on the table has no handle.

h) The candlestick on the mantel has no handle, although there is a curved line back of the chicken which suggests one.

[PLATE B]

a) There is a small *2* in the lower right corner of the rug, and there is one dot before and one after the name *PHIZ*.

b) The signature is in italic capital letters, the first and last letters with simple flourishes.

c) The child's bonnet has a long and a short string attached.

d) The lower picture shows a girl with her arm raised or with a stick in her hand.

e) There is a man in the castle archway. His arm is hanging at his side, and both of his legs show.

f) There is a liquid falling from the spoon to the cup.

g) Same as in Plate A.

h) The handle of the candlestick is a complete circle.

Emotion of Mr. Kenwigs on hearing the family news from Nicholas.

Emotion of Mr Kenwigs on hearing the family news from Nicholas.

Emotion of Mr Kenwigs on hearing the family news from Nicholas.

[PLATE C]

a) This plate is not numbered, but there are three dots in the artist's signature, one before, one following the *P*, and one after the *Z*.

b) There is a curlicue in front of the signature.

c) The strings of the bonnet are of equal length.

d) The lower picture shows two children.

e) The man in the archway of the castle seems to have but one leg and a raised arm.

f) Same as in Plate A.

g) The cup has a handle.

h) The candlestick is imperfectly drawn, and the handle does not complete the circle at the left.

Part XII · Plate 23 · Page 356

Mr. Linkinwater Intimates His Approval of Nicholas

There were four etchings of this plate, apparently not numbered, although, if the others were numbered, a vertical mark on the first might be considered the figure 1.

[P L A T E   A]

a) There is a straight vertical mark in the margin at the lower right.
b) The signature is backhand, with the Z reversed. One dot follows it.
c) The ledger over Nicholas' head has a swastika-like ornament on the front and three raised bands on the spine.
d) No faces show through the windows at the rear.
e) Between Mr. Linkinwater and the Cheeryble brothers and below the window there is no picture on the wall.
f) The right-hand page of Mr. Linkinwater's ledger shows the numeral 12 at the bottom of a series of horizontal lines.
g) The legend reads *Mr. Linkinwater intimates his approval of Nicholas.*

[P L A T E   B]

a) There is no sign of a number.
b) There is one dot before the signature, which is smaller than in Plate. A.
c) The ledger has no swastika but has five raised bands.
d) Two heads show through the window, the one at the left wearing a sou'wester.
e) Same as in Plate A.
f) There are six horizontal lines at the top of the left ledger page and a vertical line at the left.
g) Same as in Plate A.

[P L A T E   C]

a) There is no sign of a number.
b) The signature in capitals is within the shading of the floor.
c) The ledger has no swastika but has five raised bands.
d) Two heads show through the window; the one at the left has a mustache and apparently a beard, the one at the right is bald.
e) Same as in Plate A.
f) The left-hand ledger page shows several horizontal lines and vertical lines at the right and left.
g) The legend is without the "Mr." before Linkinwater's name.

[P L A T E   D]

a) There is no sign of a number.
b) The signature is in script within the shading of the floor boards.
c) The ledger has no swastika but has four raised bans.
d) The left head in the window wears a sou'wester and has a screwed-up face.
e) There is a picture of a house on the wall between Mr. Linkinwater and the Cheeryble brothers.
f) The ledger page at the left shows only horizontal scratches.
g) Same as in Plate A.

Mr. Linkinwater intimates his approval of Nicholas.

Mr. Linkinwater intimates his approval of Nicholas.

Linkinwater intimates his approval of Nicholas.

Mr. Linkinwater intimates his approval of Nicholas.

Part XII · Plate 24 · Page 373

A Sudden Recognition Unexpected on Both Sides

Etched in quadruplicate. Only Plate B is numbered.

[P L A T E   A]

a) There is no plate number.
b) The artist's signature is in backhand script at the lower center.
c) There are two coachmen in the distance between the lamppost and the fishing-tackle store.
d) The man to the right of the distant lamppost faces the left.
e) A man's head appears over the shoulder of the left hod carrier.
f) The house sign is *Fishing Tackle*.
g) The capital *I* in the sign *Seminary for Young Ladies. French by a Native* is dotted in the words *Ladies* and *Native*.
h) The word *Emporium* appears in the upper right corner.

[P L A T E   B]

a) This plate is numbered *2* twice, once below the right foot of the boy at the left and again about an inch farther to the right but below the pavement.
b) The signature is in capitals and looks like "SHIZ," with the *Z* reversed.
c) There are three coachmen in the distance.
d) The man at the right of the distant lamppost faces the right.
e) No head appears over the hod carrier's shoulder.
f) The house sign is *SHAR . . . FISHING TACKLE*.
g) The letters *I* are not dotted.
h) Same as in Plate A.

[P L A T E   C]

a) There is no plate number.
b) The signature in capitals is reversed. It looks like "SIHP," with the *P* looking like a reversed figure *2*.
c) There are two coachmen in the distance.
d) At the right of the distant lamppost there is a boy facing the left.
e) Same as in Plate B.
f) The first and last letters of *Fishing Tackle* are incomplete.
g) Same as in Plate B.
h) The word *Emporium* does not appear.

[P L A T E   D]

a) There is no plate number.
b) The signature is in capitals, with the *Z* reversed, much like that in Plate B.
c) Same as in Plate C.
d) The boy at the right of the distant lamppost has a visor on his cap.
e) Same as in Plate B.
f) The first three letters of *Fishing Tackle* are drawn in single lines.
g) Same as in Plate B.
h) Same as in Plate C.

A sudden recognition, unexpected on both sides.

A sudden recognition, unexpected on both sides.

A sudden recognition, unexpected on both sides.

A sudden recognition, unexpected on both sides.

a) The number *3* occurs below the chair as well as in the lower right corner of the paper on the desk.
b) The signature looks more like "Rniz" than "Phiz."
c) The left panel of the cabinet shows no carving, but it is shaded differently from that in Plate A.
d) There are three drawer pulls.
e) There is no box at the back.

[P L A T E   D]

a) The number *4* is shown below the leg of the chair at the right.
b) The signature is much like that in Plate C.
c) The left panel of the cabinet is carved with figures similar to Titian's "Moses in the Bullrushes."
d) There are three drawer pulls.
e) The box shows a handle similar to that in Plate B.

Part XIII · Plate 25 · Page 390

Nicholas Recognizes the Young Lady Unknown

This plate was etched four times, all but the first numbered in Arabic numerals below the rear leg of the chair at the right.

[P L A T E   A]

a) This plate is probably not numbered, although there is a vertical scratch with a dot above that looks like the letter *i* back of the chair at the right. It may be intended for the figure 1.
b) The artist's signature is in backhand, with a curve behind.
c) The left panel of the cabinet shows no carving.
d) The top two drawers of the desk show knobs.
e) The box on the stand behind the desk at the right shows a white spot for a handle.

[P L A T E   B]

a) This plate has the number *2* without an angle below the leg of the chair. What is apparently a figure 3 back of the chair is actually only part of the carving.
b) The artist's signature flows more freely than that in Plate A.
c) The left panel of the cabinet is carved only around the rectangle.
d) All three drawers in the desk have knobs.
e) The box on the stand at the right shows an oval handle.

Nicholas recognizes the Young Lady unknown.

Nicholas recognizes the Young Lady unknown.

Nicholas recognizes the Young Lady unknown

Nicholas recognizes the Young Lady unknown.

Part XIII · Plate 26 · Page 404

The Gentleman Next Door Declares His Passion
for Mrs. Nickleby

This plate was etched in quadruplicate.

[P L A T E A]

a) There is a short vertical line among the flowers at the lower left which
may possibly represent a figure 1.
b) The signature, in flowing backhand script, looks like "Ruz."
c) One of the birds in the sky at the upper left is higher up than the other.
d) There is a flower directly above the head of the gentleman next door and
another above his right elbow and lower down than the other blossoms.
e) There is only one diagonal brace extending to the front chair leg.

[P L A T E B]

a) There is a faint curved line below the flowers in the lower left margin which
may represent a figure 2, although it looks more like a script *L* reversed.
b) The signature is in unornamented backhand that looks like "Ruz."
c) Neither of the two birds' heads nor the left wing of the bird at the right
is shaded.
d) There is no flower near the gentleman's right elbow.
e) The braces for the legs of the chair form a cross.

[P L A T E C]

a) There is no sign of a number.
b) The signature is in backhand capitals. The *H* has a double cross-line.
c) The heads of the birds and the left wing of the one to the right are shaded.
d) Same as in Plate B.
e) There is only one brace.

The Gentleman next door declares his passion for M.ʳˢ Nickleby.

The Gentleman next door declares his passion for Mrs Nickleby.

The Gentleman next door declares his passion for Mrs Nickleby.

The Gentleman next door declares his passion for Mrs. Nickleby.

[PLATE D]

a) There is a faint number 4 at the margin near the flowerpots.
b) The signature is in backhand script at the lower center and looks like "Ring."
c) The birds are shaded like those in Plate B.
d) A flower touches the gentleman's right elbow.
e) Same as in Plates A and C.

Part XIV

Owing to the illness of Hablôt K. Browne, the plates for this part, together with those for the next, were issued with Part XV.

Part XV · Plate 27 · Page 435

Mr. Mantalini Poisons Himself for the Seventh Time

This plate was etched in triplicate, but only the third was numbered.

[PLATE A]

a) The signature is in backhand capitals with a short dash before it.
b) The girl at the left of the door has a bonnet tie beneath her chin. The girl at her right has a thin cord across her forehead.
c) The handrail of the banister seen through the door is clearly defined, part of the underside being shown by two lines.
d) The footman's right thumb shows below Mr. Mantalini's whiskers.
e) Mr. Mantalini's eyes appear to be very slightly open.
f) The door casing shows no cornice.

[PLATE B]

a) The signature, in backhand script, is followed by a paraph.

b) The girl near the door has no tie beneath her chin. The girl at her right has a cord as in Plate A.

c) The handrail is less clearly shown, and both lower and upper lines are single.

d) The footman's right thumb does not show.

e) Mr. Mantalini's eyes are closed.

f) The door casing has a cornice.

[PLATE C]

a) The signature is much like that in Plate A, but it is partly covered by the shading of the floor. It is followed by a figure *3*, and there is another *3* under the skirts of the girl at the right.

b) The girl near the door has a bow tie beneath her chin, but the girl at her right has no cord about her forehead.

c) The handrail is indistinct.

d) Same as in Plate B.

e) Same as in Plate B.

f) Same as in Plate B.

Mr. Mantalini poisons himself for the seventh time.

Mr Mantalini poisons himself for the seventh time.

Mr Mantalini poisons himself for the seventh time.

Mr. Snawley Enlarges on Parental Instinct

This plate was etched in triplicate. Only the second is numbered.

[P L A T E   A]

a) The signature is rather scratchy in backhand capital letters, and there is a short dash above the *I* and another below it.
b) The door casing above the door at the hinge side shows horizontal shade lines.
c) The tumbler on the table shows horizontal lines, which seem to be shade lines rather than indicating a liquid within it.
d) Browdie's pocket shows a dark button.
e) The plate is not numbered unless a short diagonal line to the left of 'Tilly Browdie's foot indicates a figure 1.

[P L A T E   B]

a) The signature is in backhand script with a dash before it.
b) The door casing shows no shading above the door.
c) The tumbler on the table is empty, but the shade lines cut through it.
d) The button on Browdie's pocket is almost invisible on account of two sets of shade lines.
e) There is a number *2* below 'Tilly's skirt.

[P L A T E   C]

a) The signature is covered by the shading of the floor.
b) The door casing shows several straight lines of dots for shading.
c) The tumbler on the table is half-full.
d) There is a white spot on Browdie's coat pocket in place of a button.
e) There is no number on the plate.

Mr Snawley enlarges on parental instinct.

Mr Snawley enlarges on parental instinct.

Mr Snawley enlarges on parental instinct.

Nicholas Makes His First Visit to the Lodgings of Mr. Bray

This plate was etched in quadruplicate, all but the first numbered.

[P L A T E   A]

a) The signature is in backhand capitals, with a dot preceding the *P*, another between the *I* and *Z*, and a third following the *Z*.
b) The legend reads: *Nicholas makes his first visit to the lodgings of Mr. Bray.*
c) Only the top and part of the sides of the two upper panels of the door are shown.
d) The foot of Mr. Bray's table is shaded with horizontal lines.
e) The top end of the bell cord consists of five perfectly straight lines, the middle one heavier than the others.
f) Madeline's dress is closed by several buttons and a straight line.
g) The plate is not numbered.

[P L A T E   B]

a) The signature is in capitals without dots.
b) The legend is the so-called "short" title: *Nicholas makes his first visit to Mr. Bray.*
c) Two top panels are shown and two sides of a third below these.
d) The foot of Mr. Bray's table is shaded mostly by vertical lines.
e) The lower end of the bell cord consists of four straight lines which merge into three above.
f) Madeline's dress is closed by two frogs and one or two buttons.
g) There is a faint number *2* at the lower left, near Madeline's foot.

[P L A T E   C]

a) The signature in script looks like "Ruz."
b) Same as in Plate A, although the length from the dot in the initial *N* to the period at the end is only 90 mm., while in Plate A it is 93.5 mm.
c) Only the top door panels are shown, but the one to the left is marked by lines on all four sides.
d) The foot of Mr. Bray's table is shaded by both horizontal and vertical lines.

Nicholas makes his first visit to the lodgings of Mr. Bray.

e) The upper end of the bell cord consists of five lines, but the lines as they continue downward are broken and not ruled.
f) Madeline's dress is closed by a double line, but neither buttons nor frogs are shown.
g) There are three short vertical lines below the footstool, representing a Roman III.

Nicholas makes his first visit to M.ʳ Bray.

Nicholas makes his first visit to the lodgings of M.ʳ Bray.

Nicholas makes his first visit to the lodgings of Mr Bray.

a) The signature is similar to that in Plate C, although the *Z* has a longer curly tail.
b) Same as in Plate C, but it is 92 mm. long.
c) Only the top lines of two panels are shown.
d) Same as in Plate C.
e) The bell cord consists of numerous freehand lines.
f) Same as in Plate C.
g) There is a Roman numeral *IIII* below the footstool.

Part XV · Plate 30 · Page 462

The Consultation

This plate was etched in quadruplicate, two of the plates numbered.

[PLATE A]

a) There is a colon or a lower-case *i* at the foot of Gride's chair, probably indicating the first plate.
b) The signature is in capitals at the lower right.
c) Only the top and bottom lines of the upper panel of the desk show.
d) The upper half-door has two panels, and the doorknob shows a shank.
e) The hat on the wall has over-all shading.
f) There is no brace between the two front legs of Gride's chair.

[PLATE B]

a) The plate number is shown by a Roman *II* below the leg of Gride's chair.

b) The signature is in script at the lower right and shows the *P* with a double loop.

c) The top panel of the desk has four lines, although three of the corners are not closed.

d) The top half of the door shows two complete panels and two that are unfinished. The doorknob has a shank.

e) The hat shows seven vertical lines of shading on top.

f) Same as in Plate A.

[PLATE C]

a) There is no number to indicate whether this is the third or fourth plate.

b) The signature is scrawled with an apostrophe over the *z.*

c) The top desk panel is drawn with double lines for the sides and single lines for the top and bottom.

d) The door shows two complete panels, and the knob shows a shank.

e) The hat shows dots for shading and a few curved lines at the left part of the cylindrical portion.

f) There is a white brace between the legs of Gride's chair.

[PLATE D]

a) Same as in Plate C.

b) The signature in script looks like "Rnz."

c) There is no top panel on the desk.

d) There are two panels to the door; the knob shows no shank.

e) The hat has dots and a few short scratchy lines for shading.

f) Same as in Plate A.

The Consultation

The Consultation.

The Consultation.

The Consultation.

Mysterious Appearance of the Gentleman
in the Small Clothes

There were four steels made of this plate. All are apparently numbered, but, unfortunately, two have marks which might indicate the third plate. Since Plates B and D clearly seem to be the second and fourth, it was necessary to decide which of the remaining two was actually the third and which the first. The plate here taken as Plate A has a small curlicue in the center of the front of the mantel which may possibly have been intended for the figure 3, just as in the same position in Plate D there is a figure 4. On the other hand, Plate B is marked in Roman numerals, and the plate here given as C is marked *III*. Apparently, the latter is actually the third, and the figure *3* on the fireplace of Plate A is just an ornament, for an inspection of the plates, when lined up as here given, shows a certain sequence of similarities. In Plate A the fans have no faces, while in Plates B, C, and D they are present. Plate A shows no ornamental carving at the bases of the uprights of the mantel mirror, while Plates B, C, and D show comparable carvings. Plates A and B have no bowknots at the tops of the bell cords at the left of the fireplace, while Plates C and D do. In Plate A Mrs. Nickleby's back hair shows dark, while in Plates B, C, and D it is covered by her cap. The knob on the fire tongs in Plate A is an acorn; in the following three it is approximately spherical. Many other similar sequences might be pointed out, all seeming to indicate that Plate A as here given should be at either one or the other end of the series, but, since Plate D is clearly marked with a *4*, that should be the last and the other the first.

[PLATE A]

a) While this plate shows a mark at the front of the mantel which might be taken for a figure 3, it is, as mentioned above, apparently only an ornament.
b) The signature is in capital letters.
c) The fans on the mantel do not show faces.
d) The bell cord at the left shows no bow at the top, but it is extended to the ceiling.
e) Mrs. Nickleby's left thumb turns into the palm of her hand.

[PLATE B]

a) This plate is marked *II* below the back leg of the chair.
b) The signature is very similar to that in Plate A.
c) The mouth of the face on the left fan seems to be saying "Oh!" The right fan smiles.
d) The bell cord at the left of the mantel shows no bow at the top. It does not reach the ceiling.
e) Mrs. Nickleby's left thumb is turned upward.

[PLATE C]

a) There is a Roman *III* at the lower left, below Mrs. Nickleby's skirt.
b) The signature is similar to that in Plates A and B, but it has a dark dot above the space between the *I* and the *Z*.
c) The fan at the left has one eye closed as if winking; the fan at the right has a lopsided mouth.
d) The bell cord at the left shows a bowknot at the top. None of the vertical lines touches the mantel.
e) Mrs. Nickleby's left thumb is turned upward.

[PLATE D]

a) There is a figure *4* in the central ornament of the mantel.
b) The *Z* of the signature is provided with flourishes at top and bottom.
c) The left fan is smiling; the right fan's mouth is a line parallel to the handle.
d) The left cord has a bow at the top. Two of the vertical lines practically reach the mantel.
e) Mrs. Nickleby's thumb is shown in front of her palm.

Mysterious appearance of the Gentleman in the small clothes.

Mysterious appearance of the Gentleman in the small clothes.

Mysterious appearance of the Gentleman in the small clothes.

Mysterious appearance of the Gentleman in the small clothes.

The Last Brawl between Sir Mulbery [*sic*] and His Pupil

Four steels were etched. Certain markings may represent numbers or may simply be ornamental lines. In all the plates the name "Mulberry" is misspelled in the legend.

[P L A T E A]

a) The plate is not numbered.
b) The signature is in capitals within the shading of the foreground. The *Z* of *PHIZ* is fancy, with loops at the top and bottom and a dot in the upper loop.
c) The man with the large red nose lying on the floor at the right has buttons on his vest along the central line only.
d) The little fingers of both hands of the Irishman standing above all the other men are extended.
e) The two cards nearest the upraised hand of the angry man at the left are an ace and a blank. (No. 1?)
f) One candle is smoking in the right chandelier and two in the left.
g) There are four dice on the floor.

[P L A T E B]

a) Below the bottle at the lower right are two straight lines within a circle. These may or may not represent the Roman numeral II.
b) The signature is somewhat similar to that in Plate A.
c) The man on the floor at the right has a row of buttons on the left side of his vest, as well as buttons along the central line.
d) The little finger of the Irishman's left hand only is extended.
e) The two cards nearest the angry man's hand are both aces. (No. 2?)
f) One candle is smoking in each chandelier.
g) There are five dice on the floor.

[P L A T E   C]

a) The card below the bottle on the floor is distinctly marked *3*.

b) The signature is similar to that in Plates A and B, except that both top and bottom curves of the *Z* are open to the left.

c) The vest of the man lying on the floor at the right seems to be embroidered.

d) As in Plate A.

e) The two cards nearest the angry man's hand are a trey and a blank. (No. 3?)

f) Two candles are smoking in the left chandelier and one in the right.

g) Same as in Plate A.

[P L A T E   D]

a) Between the legs of the overturned chair at the left there are four short parallel lines, apparently to indicate the fourth plate.

b) The signature is in capitals, with a fancy *Z*, whose loops above and below open to the right. There is a dot between the *I* and the *Z*.

c) There are no ornaments on the vest of the fallen man at the right, but the buttons are along the central line.

d) The Irishman's left little finger is extended, the right is raised from the bottle but is not extended. He is losing some of his wine.

e) The two cards nearest the hand of the angry man are a blank and a trey. If these indicate the number of the plate, there should be an ace and a trey.

f) Two candles at the left and one at the right are smoking.

g) As in Plate A.

The last brawl between Sir Mulbery and his pupil.

The last brawl between Sir Mulbery and his pupil.

The last brawl between Sir Mulbery and his pupil.

The last brawl between Sir Mulbery and his pupil.

Great Excitement of Miss Kenwigs at the Hair Dressers Shop

This very successful and well-balanced illustration was etched four times, none of which appears to be numbered.

[PLATE A]

a) This plate has no signature.
b) The windowpane below the one with the letter *N* shows something that looks like a crowned head.
c) Newman Noggs's newspaper has four columns to the page.
d) The poster back of Newman's head shows a girl with very abundant hair and the word *ROWLANDS*.
e) The lower half of the mirror to the right of the poster is shaded.
f) The top shelf and the one below show only one jar each.
g) The barber at the right has a string hanging below his apron.

[PLATE B]

a) The signature is in capitals, with only a small loop to the *Z.*
b) The windowpane below the one with the letter *N* shows something that looks like a Japanese flag.
c) Newman Noggs's paper has three columns.
d) The poster shows a smaller girl and an incomplete word *ROWLAN.*
e) The upper half of the mirror is shaded.
f) Both the top shelf and the one below show two jars.
g) Same as in Plate A.

[P L A T E   C]

a) The signature is similar to that in Plate B.
b) The windowpane below the one with the letter *N* shows a gallows(?).
c) Same as in Plate B.
d) The poster girl has lost some hair, and there is no lettering.
e) Same as in Plate B.
f) The top shelf has two jars and some shadows; the bottom shelf has one jar.
g) Same as in Plate A.

[P L A T E   D]

a) The signature is in capitals, with a fancy *Z*.
b) The window shows nothing below the *N*.
c) Same as in Plate B.
d) The girl has lost more hair, but *ROVHP* is apparently the name.
e) Same as in Plate B.
f) The top shelf has two jars, the lower shelf one.
g) There is no string dangling from the barber's apron.

Great excitement of Miss Kenwigs at the hair dressers shop.

Great excitement of Miss Kenwigs at the hair dressers shop.

Great excitement of Miss Kenwigs at the hair dressers shop.

Great excitement of Miss Kenwigs at the hair dressers shop.

Nicholas Congratulates Arthur Gride on His Wedding Morning

This plate is another example of "Phiz's" penchant for drawings that simulate stage settings. It was etched in quadruplicate, and several bear numbers.

[PLATE A]

a) This plate is not numbered.
b) The signature is in capital letters and ends in a fancy Z.
c) The vertical lines of the panels in the door are single.
d) The drawer of the dresser shown between Nicholas and his uncle has two knobs.
e) The tip of the third as well as the little finger of Gride's right hand is shown.
f) All five fingers of the glove on the floor are visible.
g) The stripes on Nicholas' vest as well as on its collar appear as double lines.
h) The stripes on the back of the chair behind Kate, beginning at the left, are shown at the top by 4, 4, and 4 lines.

[PLATE B]

a) The plate is not numbered.
b) The signature appears as in Plate A, with a dot above the Z.
c) The door panels have double lines for the verticals and single lines for the horizontals.
d) The drawer has only one knob.
e) The tip of the third finger of Gride's right hand cannot be seen.
f) Not all the fingers of the glove show.
g) Most of the stripes of Nicholas' vest are single lines, but those of the vest's collar are double.
h) The stripes on the chair show 3, 3, and 3 lines.

a) There is a number *3* after the signature.

b) The signature is in capitals, with two dots between the flourishes of the letter *Z*.

c) The door panel, whose four sides show, has double lines at the top and **on** two sides but only a single line below.

d) There is no knob on the drawer.

e) Same as in Plate B.

f) Same as in Plate B.

g) All the stripes of Nicholas' vest and some of those on its collar are single.

h) The stripes on the back of the chair are 3, 3, and 2.

[P L A T E   D]

a) There is a very faint number *4* after the signature and also two vertical lines crossed by another, looking like the same number.

b) The signature is similar to that in Plate C, although the *Z* is not so fancy. There is a dot between the *I* and the *Z*.

c) All four sides of the door panel are shown by double lines.

d) Same as in Plate B.

e) Same as in Plate B.

f) Same as in Plate B.

g) The stripes on Nicholas' vest and its collar are single except one of those on the collar.

h) The stripes on the back of the chair are 3, 3, and 2 at the upper ends.

Nicholas congratulates Arthur Gride on his Wedding Morning.

Nicholas congratulates Arthur Gride on his Wedding Morning.   *Nicholas congratulates Arthur Gride on his Wedding Morning.*

Nicholas congratulates Arthur Gride on his Wedding Morning.

Part XVIII · Plate 35 · Page 571

Mr. Squeers and Mrs. Sliderskew Unconscious
of Visitors

This plate was etched in triplicate, none of them numbered.

[P L A T E   A]

a) The *Z* of the signature has no loop at the top.
b) The dots of the shading in the upper left corner of the wall are mostly in diagonal lines.
c) The document touching Squeers's left toe has the tie on top.
d) There is no string hanging down from the bellows handle.
e) The chair with the candle shows vertical damage to the panel.
f) The broken cabinet door is damaged on the left side.
g) The corbel between the wisps of smoke shows an animal face.
h) Mrs. Sliderskew's eyes are both open.

[P L A T E   B]

a) The *Z* of the signature has loops at both top and bottom, and both are open to the right.
b) The dots of shading above Noggs's bellows are in horizontal rows.
c) The document is a short distance removed from Squeers's foot. It shows no knot in the encircling cord.
d) Same as in Plate A.
e) The chair is patched with a horizontal board.
f) The cabinet door is damaged at the bottom.
g) The corbel shows no face.
h) Mrs. Sliderskew's eyes are both open.

a) The *Z* of the signature has the top loop open to the right, the bottom one open to the left.

b) The dots of the shading above the bellows are in vertical rows.

c) The document is still farther away from Squeers's boot. It shows two tie strings.

d) A string hangs from the bellows handle.

e) The chair with the candle is undamaged.

f) The cabinet door is damaged at the bottom.

g) The corbel between the wisps of smoke shows a smiling human face.

h) Mrs. Sliderskew's right eye is almost closed in a wink.

Mr. Squeers and Mrs. Sliderskew unconscious of Visitors.

Mr Squeers and Mrs Sliderskew unconscious of Visitors.

Mr Squeers and Mrs Sliderskew unconscious of Visitors.

Part XVIII · Plate 36 · Page 574

The Recognition

This plate was etched in triplicate, all apparently numbered. There are many changed details in the shading and in the foliage.

[P L A T E A]

a) The signature is in large capitals without ornaments. There is a dot before the *P*, another above the *Z*, and a short dash under the name.

b) At the root of the tree at the right and within the grass, there is a small figure *1*.

c) The left window of the house in the background is open, and the panes are indicated by diagonally crossed lines. The opening itself is shaded by vertical lines, while the closed window at the right shows lines sloping downward to the right.

d) The vertical lines of the mattress, beginning at the left, number 2, 2, 2, and 2. None begins under Smike's forefinger.

e) The medicine glass on the table touches the mattress.

[P L A T E B]

a) The signature, in large letters, has not the Doric simplicity of that in Plate A. The *P* is in script and is joined to the *H*, so that the two together make the letter *R*. The *Z* has loops at the top and bottom, both opening to the right. There is a dot in the central angle of the *Z* and also one below the *P*.

b) At the root of the tree at the right, in the same position as the number in Plate A, there is an angular figure *2* which is more perfect upside down than right side up.

c) The open window at the left is very faintly shown. The opening itself is shaded by vertical lines. The closed window shows crossed diagonal lines.

d) The vertical lines of the mattress are in groups of 2, 3, 3, 2, and 2, the last group beginning just below Smike's finger.

e) The medicine glass does not touch the mattress.

[P L A T E C]

a) The signature is similar to that in Plate B, but it has no loop at the top of the *Z*. Below this letter the line goes back and forth several times.

b) There are three short lines at the root of the tree.

c) The opened window shows lines sloping downward to the right and only two short horizontals. The opening itself has both horizontal and vertical shade lines. The window at the right has crossed lines representing panes.

d) The vertical lines of the mattress are rather sketchily drawn but appear as 1, 3, 3, and 2, supplemented by lines of dots. There is no stripe below Smike's forefinger.

e) Same as in Plate B.

The recognition

The recognition

The recognition

The Breaking-Up of Dotheboys Hall

The List of Illustrations indicates that this plate belongs on page 615, and it was so placed in the books when bound. Actually, it should follow the one marked Plate 38. The plate numbers should be reversed, and this plate should have been inserted at page 621.

This plate was etched in triplicate. None is numbered.

[P L A T E A]

a) The signature is in backhand capitals. The *Z* is looped, and there is a dot in front of the *P*, another within the lines of the *Z*, and one after the *Z*.
b) Several recognizable letters are carved on the bench in the lower right corner. Only one leg of the bench shows.
c) The legging of the boy in the center foreground has seven buttons.
d) There is a tassel on the cap of the boy standing on the table.
e) Part of the crossbar and the door above it are shaded by vertical lines.

[P L A T E B]

a) The signature is as in Plate A. The *Z* is looped, and there is a dot over the *I*.
b) There are no recognizable letters carved on the bench.
c) Same as in Plate A.
d) Same as in Plate A.
e) The crossbar is shaded by horizontal lines and the door above it by vertical lines.

[P L A T E C]

a) The signature is similar to the preceding, but there are dots only in front of the *P* and within the *Z*.
b) Same as in Plate B.
c) There are only six buttons on the boy's legging.
d) There is no tassel on the boy's cap.
e) The crossbar is shaded by a few horizontal lines but the door above it is unshaded.

The 'breaking up' at Dotheboys Hall.

The 'breaking up' at Dotheboys Hall.

The breaking up at Dotheboys Hall.

Reduced Circumstances of Mr. Mantalini

This plate was etched in triplicate, none numbered.

[P L A T E   A]

a) The wheel of the mangle is not shown.
b) The word *Mangling* on the sign on the door is complete.
c) The rear leg of the chair between Mr. and Mrs. Mantalini extends below the crossbrace.
d) The tub below the broom at the right shows a handle.
e) The signature has a dot between the *H* and the *I*.

[P L A T E   B]

a) The mangle has a wheel.
b) The word *Mangling* on the door is incomplete.
c) The rear leg of the chair ends above the brace.
d) Same as in Plate A.
e) The signature has a dot in the *Z*.

[P L A T E   C]

a) Same as in Plate B.
b) Same as in Plate A.
c) Same as in Plate A.
d) The tub has no handle.
e) The signature has a small circle over the *I*.

Reduced circumstances of Mr. Mantalini.

Reduced circumstances of Mr. Mantalini.

Reduced circumstances of M.ʳ Mantalini

Part XX · Plate 39 · Page 624

The Children at Their Cousin's Grave

This plate was etched in triplicate.

[P L A T E A]

a) The signature is in capitals, the *Z* having a simple loop below.
b) The post at the right has no number on it, but there is a very small vertical line preceded by a dash in the margin at the lower right below the foliage. This may have been intended for the number 1.
c) There are at least five, maybe seven, birds at the left of the tower and eight or nine at the right.

[P L A T E B]

a) The signature is much like that in Plate A, but the lower part of the *Z* is confused by the spears of grass.
b) The post has no number, and nowhere else on the plate is there anything that is definitely determinable as a number.
c) There are only two birds at the left of the tower and ten, exclusive of the one far to the right, on the other side.

[P L A T E C]

a) The signature has loops above and below the *Z*.
b) The post at the right is marked *III* near the top, and there is a reversed *3* below it.
c) There are only two birds at the left of the tower, but they are flying one above the other instead of side by side, as in Plate B. There are twelve birds at the right.

168 / NICKLEBY   *Plate 38C*

The children at their cousin's grave.   *The children at their cousin's grave.*

The children at their cousin's grave

Maclise's Portrait of Charles Dickens

This portrait, engraved by Finden from a painting by D. Maclise, was made in duplicate, but they are so nearly alike that it is rather difficult to separate them. Both plates have the publishers' imprint, *London, Published Octr. 1, 1839, by Chapman & Hall, 186, Strand*, below Dickens' signature. In later impressions this is missing. However, bound copies may be so closely trimmed that only traces remain, or it may be cut off entirely. Measuring the distance between Dickens' signature and the bottom of the page will show whether there was room for it. Arbitrarily calling one of the plates A and the other B, since there is no way of telling which was engraved first and either may appear in a first edition, the following differences may be pointed out.

[P L A T E A]

a) The upper lock of Dickens' hair stands somewhat apart from the main mass, and the background pattern shows between.

b) The shading of the upper part of the arm of the chair at the right edge of the picture is almost straight, and there is no white line separating it from the upholstery.

c) The round ornament on the top of the other arm of the chair does not touch the upholstery.

d) The engraved line which forms the outline of the chair at the left, if continued downward, would end over the letter *M* of *Maclise*.

e) The distance from the lowest point of the *D* in *Dickens* in the signature, to the top of the lower-case letters in the publishers' imprint is 19 mm.

[PLATE B]

a) The top lock of Dickens' hair curves downward to touch the main mass.

b) The shading of the upper part of the arm of the chair under Dickens' left arm shows a distinct curve at the end, and there is a white line separating it from the upholstery.

c) The round ornament on the other arm touches the upholstery.

d) The engraved line which forms the back of the chair, if continued downward, would end over *te* of the word *Painted*.

e) The distance between the lowest point of the *D* and the top of the lower-case letters of the publishers' imprint is $16\frac{1}{2}$ mm.

Both plates have been retouched, and slight differences may be found.

Faithfully yours

Charles Dickens

London, Published Oct. 1, 1839, by Chapman & Hall, 186, Strand.

The
Life and Adventures
of
MARTIN CHUZZLEWIT

Following *Nicholas Nickleby* came *Master Humphrey's Clock*, containing *The Old Curiosity Shop* and *Barnaby Rudge*. It appeared in weekly parts from April, 1840, to November, 1841, and these, every fourth or fifth week, were combined to make twenty monthly parts. Since the engravings were woodcuts and all appeared in the text except the 3 frontispieces for the bound volumes, no duplicates were made; consequently, they do not come within the scope of the present work, even though 2 of the frontispieces, 130 of the woodcuts, and 25 initial letters were by Hablôt K. Browne.

The next major work by Dickens which appeared with duplicate or triplicate etched plates was *Martin Chuzzlewit*. This was published by Chapman and Hall in London and came out in twenty monthly parts, similar to *Pickwick* and *Nickleby*— the first part in January, 1843, and the last in July, 1844. Two illustrations were issued with each part, and, as before, they were etched on quarto steels with two subjects on each. Duplicate plates were issued for each illustration except Plates 1, 2, 3, 4, 5, 6, 27, 28, 39, and 40, which were issued in triplicate, making a total of 90 plates. Many of them show either Arabic or Roman numerals which may possibly represent the order in which the steels were etched, but since, like *Nicholas Nickleby*, they were printed simultaneously and later cut apart and bound up indiscriminately, first editions of the book may contain any combinations of them.

Between the completion of *Nicholas Nickleby* in October, 1839, and the beginning of *Martin Chuzzlewit* in January, 1843, Browne drew at least 175 designs for woodcuts, of which 159 were for *Master Humphrey's Clock* (*Old Curiosity Shop* and *Barnaby Rudge*), and etched 158 steels. These include 10 for Theodore Hook's *Precept and Practice*, 40 for W. J. Neale's *Paul Periwinkle*, 12 for Mrs. Trollope's *Charles Chesterfield*, 44 for Lever's *Charles O'Malley*, 52 for B. C. Pelham's *Chronicles of Crime*, and 26 for Thomas Miller's *Godfrey Malvern*. And during the time that *Martin Chuzzlewit* was being issued, his industry was just as great. Besides the 90 original and duplicate plates for this novel, he etched at least 90 others, including 28 for G. P. R. James's *Commissioner; or De lunatico inquirendo*, and 45 for Lever's *Jack Hilton*. One marvels after this tremendous output that Browne's originality was not completely used up!

Meekness of Mr Pecksniff and his charming daughters.   *Meekness of Mr. Pecksniff, and his charming daughters.*

Meekness of Mr. Pecksniff and his charming daughters.

Meekness of Mr. Pecksniff and His Charming Daughters

This plate was etched in triplicate. All three show similar, but very unusual, signatures of the artist.

[P L A T E   A]

a) The poor box on the mantel is not lettered, but there is a dot on its door.

b) The picture of Pecksniff above the mantel shows no plans in his hand.

c) The large design for a monument is labeled *Design by Peksnife*. The supporting columns are plain, and the part between them is a shaded truncated cone. The figure at the top has a Napoleonic pose.

d) Tom Pinch's vest shows stripes, and his trousers are light.

e) The ornaments at the tops of the two right-hand picture cords are white.

f) A few short rays extend from the candle flame.

g) To the right of Mr. Pecksniff's left shoelace there is a short vertical line which may have been intended as the number 1.

[P L A T E   B]

a) The poor box is inscribed *Poor Box*. There are a few short vertical lines below two dots on the door.

b) There is a roll of plans in the hand of Pecksniff in the picture.

c) The picture of the monument is labeled in a single line *Peksniff, fecit, A.D. 1841*. The supporting columns show right and left twists.

d) Tom Pinch's vest is shaded but shows no stripes, and his trousers are entirely shaded by vertical lines.

e) The picture-cord ornaments are shaded.

f) There are six long rays extending out from the candle flame.

g) In the shading of the floor below Mercy's skirt and near the margin of the plate there is a mark which consists of a pointed loop and a short horizontal line to the left. It may have been a reversed figure 2 which was made unrecognizable by the extra line at the right.

a) The poor box is so lettered, but there are no dots on the door.
b) Same as in Plate B.
c) The clock monument is labeled in one line *Pecksnife, fecit*. The supporting columns show right-hand twists.
d) Same as in Plate B.
e) Same as in Plate B.
f) There are no rays from the candle.
g) Following the signature there is a reversed *3*, and there is a very faint figure *3*, also reversed, in the margin below Mercy's skirt.

Part I · Plate 2 · Page 24

Martin Chuzzlewit Suspects the Landlady without Any Reason

This plate was etched in triplicate. The first and second plates are not numbered, the third may be.

[P L A T E   A]

a) The signature in the lower right corner is indecipherable.
b) The knot of the drapery of the bed forms a hexagon.
c) Martin's pen is shaded on the right side.
d) There is no number on the plate.

[P L A T E   B]

a) The signature in the lower right corner looks like the Greek letters phi and sigma, the latter reversed, consequently *Phs*.
b) The knot of the drapery is nearly square, with the sides vertical and horizontal.
c) Martin's pen is entirely unshaded.
d) There is no number on the plate.

[P L A T E   C]

a) The signature is in script, ending with some hieroglyphics, the last of which is the astronomical symbol for Mars or the biological symbol for male.
b) The knot of the drapery is diamond-shaped.
c) Martin's pen is shaded on the left side.
d) There is a reversed *3* at the lower left, but it is very faint.

Martin Chuzzlewit suspects the landlady, without any reason.

Martin Chuzzlewit suspects the landlady, without any reason.

Martin Chuzzlewit suspects the landlady, without any reason.

Pleasant little family party at M.ʳ Pecksniff's   *Pleasant little family party at M.ʳ Pecksniff's.*

Pleasant little family party at M.ʳ Pecksniff's

Pleasant Little Family Party at Mr. Pecksniff's

This plate was etched in triplicate, each numbered in the lower left corner.

[P L A T E A]

a) The signature is in capital letters, the *Z* ending in an irregular line to the left. There are dots before the *P* and above the *I*.

b) The plate is numbered by a single short horizontal line at the left of the piano stool.

c) No line connects Mr. Pecksniff's shirt studs. His vest shows only one button and that near the top.

d) Mercy's necklace has a distinct cross attached. Her right arm does not show below the elbow. Her mouth is open.

e) The wings of the crow are unbroken.

f) There are a few sketchy lines back of the left elbow of the bald-headed man at the right which may represent a bonnet.

[P L A T E B]

a) The signature is in capitals, with a loop in front of the *P* and with the tail of the *Z* ending in a paraph below the signature.

b) The plate number is indicated by two short horizontal lines to the left of the piano stool and below the handbag.

c) A line connects three studs in Mr. Pecksniff's shirt, and his vest shows buttons all the way down.

d) Mercy's necklace shows a cross attached, her right arm does not show below the elbow, and her mouth still says "Oh!"

e) The left wing of the crow is broken across, showing only a bit of the tip to the right of the break.

f) There is nothing back of the bald-headed man's elbow.

a) The signature is in capital letters, ending in a *Z* which has loops at the top and bottom. There is a dot above the *H*.

b) The plate number is indicated by three short lines to the left of the base of the piano stool as well as by the number *3* after the signature.

c) A line connects only the upper two of Mr. Pecksniff's shirt studs, and his vest shows only suggestions of buttons.

d) Mercy's necklace has no cross attached, her right arm shows from the elbow to the wrist, and she is smiling.

e) Same as in Plate A.

f) Same as in Plate B.

Part II · Plate 4 · Page 58

Pinch Starts Homeward with the New Pupil

This plate was etched in triplicate. Many differences are to be found in the shading and so on, but they are difficult to describe in words.

[P L A T E   A]

a) The signature is in the lower right corner in capital letters with flourishes.

b) After the signature there is a line, slightly curved at the top, which apparently was intended to represent the figure 1.

c) The hook for the checkrein on the collar of the horse is turned the wrong way.

d) The bottom of the tub at the right is shaded on the lower left side.

[P L A T E   B]

a) The signature has flourishes, but they differ from those in Plate A.

b) The plate number, *II*, is in front of the signature.

c) The hook for the checkrein is turned backward, as it should be.

d) The bottom of the tub is shaded across the entire lower half.

[P L A T E   C]

a) The signature has still more flourishes.

b) There is no number on the plate.

c) Same as in Plate B.

d) The bottom of the tub is entirely unshaded.

Pinch starts homeward with the new Pupil

Pinch starts homeward with the new Pupil.

Pinch starts homeward with the new Pupil.

Mr. Pinch and the New Pupil on a Social Occasion

These steels were etched in triplicate, each marked with a number in Roman numerals. Pecksniff's name is still misspelled in the framed drawings on the walls.

[P L A T E   A]

a) The number *I* appears below the tablecloth at the right.
b) There is a smile on the face of the bust of Pecksniff, and his eyes are modestly cast down.
c) There is a poker near Martin's left leg.
d) The candle back of Tom Pinch shows radiating beams.
e) The wainscoting back of the candle is shown by two lines, one of which passes through the candle. Below these the top of a panel is shown at the right.
f) Both picture cords practically reach the frames.

[P L A T E   B]

a) The plate is numbered twice; a reversed *2* follows the signature, and a Roman *II* is near the rug at the lower left edge.
b) The eyes of the bust are apparently open, but the face is shaded.
c) Same as in Plate A.
d) Same as in Plate A.
e) The wainscoting is shown by two lines and a third a short distance below. None of the lines passes through the candle. There is no panel at the right.
f) Only the second picture cord reaches the frame.

[P L A T E   C]

a) Below and at the left of the hassock is the number *III*.
b) The eyes of the bust turn toward its right.
c) There is no poker.
d) The candle flame is shown without beams.
e) There is no wainscoting.
f) Neither picture cord reaches its frame.

Mr Pinch and the new pupil, on a social occasion.

Mr Pinch and the new pupil, on a social occasion.

Mr Pinch and the new pupil, on a social occasion.

Part III · Plate 6 · Page 88

Mark Begins To Be Jolly under Creditable Circumstances

This plate was engraved in triplicate. Plates B and C are definitely numbered. Note that the word "parlor" has the American spelling.

[PLATE A]

a) There is a tulip—or something—after the signature, which may represent the number 1.
b) The signature is in capitals, spelled *PHIIZ*. There are dots below the *P* and over the *I*.
c) There are four birds in the space between the two groups of chimneys.
d) The sign above Mark's hat reads, with some breaks, *This lane leads Salisbury.*
e) Above the leaded-glass windows over the upstanding horseshoe is the word *Parlor.*
f) The signboard shows a dragon.

[PLATE B]

a) A figure *2* follows the signature.
b) The signature reads *PHIIZ*, with a dot over the *I*. The *Z* and the *P* have flourishes.
c) There are no birds to the right of the church steeple.
d) The sign above Mark's hat reads *Leading to Salisbury.*
e) The word *Parlor* has disappeared.
f) Same as in Plate A.

[PLATE C]

a) A figure *3* follows the signature.
b) The signature is in plain capitals with dots before the *P* and between the *H* and *I*.
c) There are two birds where in Plate A there were four, but here there is also one roosting on the right-hand chimney.
d) The sign above Mark's hat reads *Nerest [sic] way Salisbury.*
e) Same as in Plate B.
f) There is no figure on the signboard.

Mark begins to be jolly, under creditable circumstances.

Mark begins to be jolly under creditable circumstances.

Mark begins to be jolly, under creditable circumstances

Part IV · Plate 7 · Page 103

M. Todgers and the Pecksniffs Call upon Miss Pinch

This plate was etched in duplicate.

[P L A T E A]

a) The signature is in plain capital letters with a dot before the *P* and over the *I*.
b) Mr. Pecksniff's shirt shows only one stud, and his vest is shaded by vertical lines.
c) One series of lines on Mrs. Todgers' purse is single, the other in pairs.
d) The roll of music above the mirror shows only a single staff.

[P L A T E B]

a) The signature is similar to that in Plate A, but there is a small circle above the space between the *H* and the *I*.
b) Mr. Pecksniff's shirt shows two studs, and his vest is shaded by vertical and diagonal lines into a dice pattern.
c) Both sets of lines on Mrs. Todgers' purse are single.
d) The roll of music shows the beginnings of numerous staffs.

M. Todgers and the Pecksniffs, call upon Miss Pinch.

M. Todgers and the Pecksniffs, call upon Miss Pinch.

Truth Prevails and Virtue Is Triumphant

This plate was etched in duplicate, the second one numbered.

[PLATE A]

a) The signature is in capital letters, with a relatively plain *Z*. It is within the shading of the floor at the lower right.
b) The plate is not numbered.
c) The lower pane of glass in the window shows cracks.
d) The door back of Charity shows a knob and a keyhole but no escutcheon plate.
e) To the right of Pecksniff's head there are three cards in the frame of the mirror.
f) There is nothing hanging on the wall between the doorknob and the mantel.
g) The buttons on Pecksniff's vest are represented by only one black dot.
h) Mercy's slipper does not show crossed straps.
i) The two buttons on old Martin's coat are dark.

[PLATE B]

a) The signature is in capital letters and ends in a fancy *Z*.
b) A figure *2* follows the signature, and there is a Roman *II* below Mercy's skirt at the left.
c) There are cracks in the next-to-the-bottom pane of glass.
d) The door shows a knob, a keyhole, and an escutcheon plate.
e) There is but one card in the frame of the mirror to the right of Pecksniff.
f) There is something hanging by a string near the mantel.
g) Pecksniff's vest shows four buttons.
h) Mercy's slipper has crossed ties.
i) Martin's coat buttons are white.

Truth prevails and Virtue is triumphant.

Truth prevails and Virtue is triumphant.

Part V · Plate 9 · Page 138

Mr. Jonas Chuzzlewit Entertains His Cousins

This plate was etched in duplicate, the second plate numbered.

M: Jonas Chuzzlewit entertains his cousins.

[P L A T E   A]

a) The signature in capital letters looks like "RHIZ." The *Z* ends in a flourish, and there is a dot between the *I* and the *Z*.
b) The plate is not numbered.
c) Chuffey's head covering shows no drawing upon it.
d) The upper box on the safe shows three locks.
e) The card on the table nearest Jonas' elbow is a face card.
f) The columns in Mercy's newspaper are separated by double lines, and both her feet show.

[P L A T E   B]

a) The signature is in capitals, with a dot over the *I* and more flourishes to the *Z* than in Plate A.
b) There is a faint number *2* shown to the right of the signature.
c) Chuffey's head covering has a face drawn upon it.
d) The upper box on the safe has only one lock.
e) The card near Jonas' *elbow* is a deuce.
f) The columns in the *Times* are separated by single lines, and only one of Mercy's feet shows.

Mr Jonas Chuzzlewit entertains his cousins.

Part V · Plate 10 · Page 160

Mr. Pecksniff Renounces the Deceiver

This plate was etched in duplicate, the second one numbered.

[PLATE A]

a) The signature at the lower left is in capitals, with a single dot over the *I* and possibly one below it. There are few flourishes.
b) The picture of Pecksniff on the mantel shows a light-colored cravat. The pump below has the spout slanting upward.
c) The pans in the scales are even.
d) The book at the left of the bust is unmarked.
e) The molding of the wainscot behind Pecksniff's head consists of three lines only. The panel below is indicated by parallel lines on three sides.

[PLATE B]

a) The plain signature at the lower left is followed by a number *2*.
b) The cravat is dark. The pump's spout is horizontal.
c) The right pan of the scales is lower than the left.
d) The book at the left of the bust is marked *Pecksnif . . . Foundati. . . . .*
e) The top of the wainscot has four lines, but the panel is shown by only two parallel lines at the top.

Mr. Pecksniff renounces the deceiver. *Mr. Pecksniff renounces the deceiver.*

Part VI · Plate 11 · Page 166

Martin Meets an Acquaintance at the House of a Mutual Relation

This plate was etched in duplicate, apparently without numbers, although certain lines may be construed as such.

[P L A T E   A]

a) The signature in plain capitals is *RHIZ*. The *Z* is large and fancy, and there is a dot after it and another over the *H*.
b) There is no letter on any of the three balls on the door.
c) The clock above the door is ruled with vertical lines.
d) There is a ticket under the cord tying the bundle lying in front of Martin's booth.
e) The upper part of the belly of the viola in the hands of the man in the right booth is unshaded.

[P L A T E   B]

a) The signature is similar to that in Plate A. It has a small circle over the *H*.
b) The upper balls of the trademark on the door show the letters *I* and *C*.
c) The clock above the door is ruled with horizontal lines.
d) There is no ticket under the cord of the bundle lying in front of Martin.
e) The belly of the viola is uniformly shaded.

Martin meets an acquaintance, at the house of a mutual relation.

Martin meets an acquaintance at the house of a mutual relation.

Part VI · Plate 12 · Page 178

Mr. Tapley Acts Third Party with Great Discretion

This plate was etched in duplicate. The day was described by Dickens as "raw, damp, dark, and dismal; the clouds were as muddy as the ground; and the short perspective of every street and avenue, was closed up by the mist as by a filthy curtain." This weather condition is hardly fulfilled by the etching.

[PLATE A]

a) The signature, in capitals, is rather scratchy, so that it is impossible to say whether a short mark at the left of it was or was not intended to be the figure 1.
b) There are seven or eight buttons on Mark's right legging.
c) Martin's left hand is unshaded, and the stitching of this glove does not show.
d) The trunk of the tree back of Martin is only lightly shaded.
e) There are four pinnacles on the right tower of the church.

[PLATE B]

a) The signature has a curve over the *H* and a flourish after the *Z* which ends below the *P.* In front there are marks which look like the letters D.S. Below the signature is the figure *2.*
b) There are ten buttons on Mark's legging.
c) The glove on Martin's left hand is shaded.
d) The trunk of the tree is quite dark.
e) There are three pinnacles and a straight vertical line above the right church tower.

Tapley acts Third Party, with great discretion.

Mr *Tapley acts Third Party, with great discretion.*

Part VII · Plate 13 · Page 199

Mr. Jefferson Brick Proposes an Appropriate Sentiment

This illustration reflects Dickens' opinion of the Americans of his day. I rather think that Martin Chuzzlewit's selfishness was a worse trait than Jefferson Brick's nationalism, which was rampant in the latter half of the nineteenth century, although it seems to be at a discount at the present time. As for the Colonel's title, he showed no greater vanity than do certain persons who, simply because they are members of various societies, let half the alphabet trail their names.

[PLATE A]

a) The signature in the lower right corner is in plain capitals, with a dot before the *P* and another over the *H*.
b) The poster of the *Rowdy Journal* on the wall back of Martin reads *Important Disclosuree's*, but the first word is crossed out and the second *E* of the next word is partly changed to an *S*.
c) The little finger of Martin's right hand is extended, but his left is not.
d) The papers on the floor show several abortive letters.
e) The shading of Colonel Diver's trousers is lengthwise.
f) Jefferson Brick's cravat is short.
g) The two books nearest the *Slang Dictionary* are lightly shaded.

[PLATE B]

a) The signature has a dot above the *H* and a fancy *Z*. The number *2* follows, and there are also two short horizontal lines, apparently a Roman *II* lying sidewise, at the left.
b) The word *important* on the poster is not crossed out, and between the final *E* and the *S* of the word *Disclosurers* there is a curved line that may be intended for an *R*.
c) The little finger of Martin's right hand is curved downward, and that of his left hand is partly extended.
d) There are no letters on the papers on the floor.
e) The shading on the Colonel's trousers is diagonal.
f) Jefferson Brick wears a flowing tie.
g) The two books nearest the dictionary are shaded.

Mr. Jefferson Brick proposes an appropriate sentiment.

Mr. Jefferson Brick proposes an appropriate sentiment.

Mr. Tapley Succeeds in Finding a "Jolly" Subject for Contemplation

This plate was etched in duplicate, neither one numbered. Poor Mark! He has not only his own troubles but must shoulder Martin's as well.

[PLATE A]

a) The signature is in capitals, with a dot before it and another over the *I*. It is spelled *RHIZ*.
b) The name *Mark Tapley* on the office door has most of the letters made with double strokes.
c) There is no keyhole in the door.
d) There is a strap with a buckle at the end of the trunk upon which the black man is sitting.
e) The jackknife near Mark's elbow lies at right angles to his arm.
f) There are two nails showing in the end of the lid of the tall trunk.

[PLATE B]

a) The signature is similar to the preceding, but the dots are above and after it.
b) Mark's name is in letters formed by single strokes.
c) There is a keyhole in the door and, above and to the right of it, a small circle.
d) There is no strap on the trunk.
e) A rudimentary jackknife lies near Mark's elbow but is parallel to his arm.
f) There are three nails in the lid of the tall trunk.

Mr. Tapley succeeds in finding a "jolly" subject for contemplation.

Tapley succeeds in finding a "jolly" subject for contemplation.

Part VIII · Plate 15 · Page 232

The Dissolution of Partnership

This plate was etched in duplicate, the second one numbered.

[P L A T E   A]

a) There is no number on the plate, and the dots in the signature are not clearly shown.
b) The back of the overturned chair is not shaded.
c) There is a button on Pecksniff's vest just below the collar.
d) The desk below the books is shaded only with vertical lines.
e) The line of the floor board below the signature is double.

[P L A T E   B]

a) The plate is numbered with a faint *2* below the back of the chair at the left.
b) The back of the overturned chair is shaded.
c) There is no button below the collar of Pecksniff's vest.
d) The desk is shaded at the left by vertical and horizontal lines.
e) The lowest line of the floor is single.

The dissolution of Partnership

The dissolution of Partnership

Mr. Pecksniff on His Mission

This plate was etched in duplicate, the second plate numbered. In spite of its crowded appearance, this is a good plate both in drawing and in etching. Browne's ability to avoid making the faces all alike is well shown.

[P L A T E   A]

a) The signature *RHIZ* has a dot before it and one over the *H*.
b) The bird in the cage faces the right.
c) Under the shelf upon which the cage stands is the word *Hairdresser*.
d) The woman with her hair in curlpapers below the good-looking girl in the doorway wears a wedding ring.
e) The child in the center of the group of children in the lower right does not wear a flowing tie.
f) The word *Easy* of *Easy Shaving* on the window is divided by the mullion between the *S* and the *Y*.

[P L A T E   B]

a) The signature shows a small circle in front of it. It reads *RHZ*, with the *Z* ending in a line to the left that has a small loop below the *H* and a hook at the end. There is a small number *2*, very faint, on a paving block in the lower left corner of the plate.
b) The bird in the cage faces the left.
c) There is no lettering under the shelf.
d) The woman who will soon need Mrs. Gamp's services wears no wedding ring.
e) The child in the center of the group at the lower right wears a flowing tie.
f) The word *Easy* is divided betwen the *A* and the *S*.

Mr. Pecksniff on his Mission.

The Thriving City of Eden as It Appeared on Paper

This plate was etched in duplicate, the second plate numbered. In the present day and age, Martin would be a good prospect for the purchase of Canadian gold-mining stock or the Brooklyn Bridge. No western American city would be deliberately laid out with irregular streets as shown on the map.

[P L A T E   A]

a) The plate is not numbered.

b) The artist's signature is in plain capitals, with dots before and above it.

c) The lower book on the desk is lettered *Ledger*, the last two letters rather rudimentary.

d) The "sort of young bayonet that flew out of his knife when he touched a spring" reaches Scadder's mouth.

e) Below the word *EDEN* at the bottom of the map are letters explanatory of the location of the police, church, etc.

[P L A T E   B]

a) There is a faint number *2* below the rock next to the ammonite in the lower right corner.

b) The signature is similar to the preceding, but dots are not determinable because of many dots in the floor.

c) There is no lettering on the ledger.

d) The toothpick does not extend to Scadder's mouth.

e) There is no lettering below the word *EDEN*.

The thriving City of Eden as it appeared on paper.

The thriving City of Eden, as it appeared on paper.

Part IX · Plate 18 · Page 288

The Thriving City of Eden as It Appeared in Fact

This plate was etched in duplicate, the second plate numbered.

[PLATE A]

a) The signature has a small circle over the *I.*
b) The plate has no number.
c) There is a pencil on the stump near the compass.
d) In the roof of the cabin, back of Mark's neck, the end of only one pole shows.

[PLATE B]

a) The *Z* of the signature has more flourishes than that in Plate A.
b) There is a faint number *2* under the point of land below the bird at the lower right.
c) There is no pencil near the compass on the stump.
d) The ends of three poles show in the roof of the cabin.

The thriving City of Eden, as it appeared in fact.

The thriving City of Eden, as it appeared in fact.

Part X · Plate 19 · Page 296

Balm for the Wounded Orphan

This plate was etched in duplicate, the second one numbered.

[P L A T E   A]

a) The signature is in plain capitals, with dots before and above it.
b) The tower in the picture to the right of Pecksniff's bust shows a cross at the top.
c) There is a stud in Tom Pinch's shirt front.
d) The leg of Charity's chair is not shaded.
e) Jonas' vest is checkered.

[P L A T E   B]

a) The signature is not clear. It is followed by a small and very faint *2*.
b) The tower shows battlements but no cross.
c) There is no stud in Tom's shirt.
d) The leg of Charity's chair is shaded.
e) Jonas' vest is plain.

Balm for the wounded orphan

Balm for the wounded orphan.

Part X · Plate 20 · Page 320

Mrs. Gamp Has Her Eye on the Future

This plate was etched in duplicate, but only the second is numbered.

[P L A T E   A]

a) The signature is in italic capitals, with a scrawled *Z*. The final line passes under the signature and then, with a reversed loop, ends in a short, straight line which makes a right-angled turn.
b) Mrs. Gamp's candle is dripping.
c) The cross-stripes of Jonas' trousers are single lines.
d) The card on the mantel has two columns.

[P L A T E   B]

a) The signature is similar to that in Plate A, but it is followed by a very small figure *2*.
b) Mrs. Gamp's candle is not dripping.
c) The cross-stripes of Jonas' trousers are double lines.
d) The card on the mantel has a single column only.

Mrs Gamp has her eye on the future.

Mrs Gamp has her eye on the future.

Part XI · Plate 21 · Page 327

The Board.

This plate was etched in duplicate.

[P L A T E   A]

a) The signature is similar to that in Plate B, but above it is a small, dark, curved line which resembles a figure 2 with the loop at the upper end joined to the stem. It is doubtful whether this is the plate number; more likely it is a mark above the *I* as part of the signature.
b) The medical officer's shirt has only the trace of a stud in it.
c) Mr. Crimple's vest is fancy, and his chair below the seat shows only two parallel lines.

[P L A T E   B]

a) The signature has a small circle over the *I*, and there is a very faint *2* below the back leg of Tigg's chair.
b) The medical officer has a stud in his shirt front.
ç) Mr. Crimple's vest shows no embroidery. His chair is shaded below the seat.

The Board.

The Board.

Easy Shaving

This plate was etched in duplicate, the second plate numbered.

[P L A T E   A]

a) The signature is covered in part by the shading of the floor. There is no number, but dots before and above the name seem to be part of the signature.

b) At the lower left there is a framed picture of a girl with hair to her knees, and below her is the word *Macassar*, indicating the power of macassar oil to grow hair.

c) Mr. Bailey's neckcloth has both vertical and horizontal lines. (Actually Mr. Bailey had divested himself of his neckcloth before sitting down.)

d) Mr. Poll's neckcloth is light.

e) The bird in the large central cage has its tail down.

[P L A T E   B]

a) The signature is entirely within the shading of the floor. There is a number *2* below the coop containing the guinea pig.

b) At the lower left the picture has been replaced by a framed poster reading: *Shaving for the Million. Shaving made Easy.* The macassar girl has been removed to the lower right behind the guinea-pig's coop.

c) Mr. Bailey's neckcloth has double vertical lines.

d) Mr. Poll's neckcloth is moderately dark.

e) The bird in the cage above Poll's head has its tail up.

Easy Shaving.

Easy Shaving.

Part XII · Plate 23 · Page 384

Mr. Moddle Is Both Particular and Peculiar in His Attentions

This plate was etched in duplicate, the second plate numbered. Neither plate is signed.

[P L A T E   A]

a) The plate is not numbered unless a little vertical line at the right of the chair is intended for the figure 1.
b) The center of the mirror shows three sets of short, parallel, horizontal lines.
c) Charity's left mitt shows two lines at the knuckles of her hand.
d) The chair at the lower right has a dark seat, and the stripes of the upholstery are fairly dark.

[P L A T E   B]

a) The number 2 is very small and faint below the leg of the chair at the lower right.
b) There is a circle in the center of the mirror.
c) Charity's mitt shows a single line at her knuckles.
d) The chair and its stripes at the lower right are fairly light.

Mr. Moddle is both particular and peculiar in his attentions.

Mr. Moddle is both particular and peculiar in his attentions.

Mr. Pecksniff Discharges a Duty Which He Owes to Society

While the List of Illustrations gives the page for this illustration as 387 and it is incorrectly inserted in the bound volume at this page, it should be 376; consequently, it is actually Plate 23, and "Mr. Moddle and Charity," now given as Plate 23, should be Plate 24.

This plate was etched in duplicate, the second one numbered.

[PLATE A]

a) The artist's signature is entirely within the shading of the ground.
b) The plate is not numbered.
c) The man in the tam-o'-shanter has the index finger of his left hand turned downward.
d) Tom Pinch's overcoat has four buttons, plus two on his sleeve.
e) Mr. Pecksniff looks like a typical megalomaniac.

[PLATE B]

a) The signature is similar to that in Plate A, but the final line of the *Z* is longer and extends beyond the *P*.
b) There is a small *2* below the foot of the boy at the left.
c) The man in the tam-o'-shanter seems to be snapping his fingers.
d) Tom Pinch's overcoat has only three buttons, plus two on the sleeve.
e) Mr. Pecksniff still looks like the same man.

Mr Pecksniff discharges a duty which he owes to Society.

Mr Pecksniff discharges a duty which he owes to Society.

Part XIII · Plate 25 · Page 386

Mr. Tapley Is Recognized by Some Fellow-Citizens of Eden

This plate was etched in duplicate, neither plate numbered. This is a good picture of a shiftless family.

[P L A T E   A]

a) The signature is partly covered by the lines of the ground.
b) Nailheads show along all four edges of the front end of the trunk.
c) Mark's right legging shows buttons at the side.

[P L A T E   B]

a) The signature is similar to that in Plate A, but the Z has a longer flourish, and there is a dot or a small circle after it.
b) The trunk shows no nailheads at the end, except three at the top.
c) Mark's right legging shows no buttons.

Mr. Tapley is recognized by some fellow-citizens of Eden.

Mr Tapley is recognized by some fellow-citizens of Eden.

Martin Is Much Gratified by an Imposing Ceremony

This plate was etched in duplicate, neither one numbered.

[P L A T E   A]

a) The signature is plain, with a small dot before it and another above.
b) The setting maul is directly over the signature.
c) The scroll under Pecksniff's arm is marked with his name, and the open plan in his hand shows the entrance to the court at the bottom.
d) The "Member for the Gentlemanly Interest" has a flowered vest and a stickpin in his cravat.

[P L A T E   B]

a) The signature is similar to that in Plate A, but with no dots.
b) The setting maul lies to the left of the signature.
c) The scroll under Mr. Pecksniff's arm shows no name, and the plan in his hand shows the entrance to the court at the top.
d) The "Member for the Gentlemanly Interest" has a plain vest and no stickpin.

Martin is much gratified by an imposing ceremony.

Martin is much gratified by an imposing ceremony.

a) The *Z* of the signature has curves at top and bottom, the lower line cutting back across the whole word.

b) There is but one bird in the sky, and its left wing ends in a sharp hook.

c) There are nailheads along the top of the bottom part of the trunk near the postboy, and the lid has only three nails.

d) The uprights of Mrs. Lupin's chair are partly light and partly dark. The dark patch at the side of the cart shows no letters.

e) There is a patch of sunlight on Tom's knee. The shading above that is in two direction.

f) Same as in Plate A.

g) Same as in Plate A.

h) In the legend the *s* was omitted from *departs*.

[P L A T E C]

a) The *Z* of the signature has curves at the top and bottom, but the latter is shorter than that in Plate B and is open to the left. There is a dot in the upper loop and one after the signature.

b) There is one bird in the sky. Its left wing is formed by a double line.

c) The trunk is similar to that in Plate A.

d) One upright of Mrs. Lupin's chair is dark and one partly dark. There is no sharply defined rectangular plate at the side of the cart, but only some vertical shade lines.

e) There is a patch of sunlight on Tom's knee. The shade lines above that are in one direction only.

f) There are no background hills.

g) The cigar of the man at the upper left has gone dead.

h) The legend is correct.

Part XIV · Plate 27 · Page 419

Mr. Pinch Departs To Seek His Fortune

This plate was etched in triplicate. It is a good picture, with a curious error in the legend in the second plate.

[P L A T E A]

a) The signature is without flourishes but has dots before the *F* and above the *I*.

b) There are two birds in the sky.

c) The trunk below the postboy's horn shows no nailheads along the joint below the lid; the lid itself has four nails.

d) The left upright of the back of Mrs. Lupin's chair is dark, and the side of the cart shows the word *Lupin* in a darkly shaded rectangle.

e) There is no light patch on Tom's knee. The trousers are shaded by nearly vertical lines.

f) Above the tasseled hat of the boy on top of the coach, two lines represent hills in the background.

g) There is smoke coming from the cigar of the man at the extreme upper left.

h) The legend is correct.

Mr Pinch departs to seek his fortune.

Mr Pinch depart to seek his fortune.

Mr Pinch departs to seek his fortune.

Mr. Nadgett Breathes, as Usual, an Atmosphere of Mystery

This plate should be inserted at page 446, although the List of Illustrations gives it as 448. It was etched in triplicate.

[PLATE A]

a) The signature has few flourishes.
b) There is a white spot within Mr. Nadgett's coattails.
c) The Pecksniffian Buddha's mouth is a straight line.
d) The fender shows no ornamentation.
e) Jonas' vest is slightly ornamented.
f) The fingers of the glove at Jonas' feet are dark.
g) The stem of the boot hook is dark.
h) The ornament on the back of Mr. Tigg's brush looks like a figure 8 with some shading below.
i) There are no letters or numbers on the side of the tablecloth. The plate is not numbered.

[PLATE B]

a) The signature is similar to that in Plate A, except that the final line of the *Z* crosses the stem.
b) Mr. Nadgett's coattails show a moderately shaded spot between them.
c) The Buddha smiles, but there is a cross-line through the hair which gives the impression that he is wearing a pointed cap.
d) There is some ornamentation on the fender.
e) Similar to that in Plate A.
f) The gloves have white fingers.
g) The stem of the boot hook is dark.
h) Mr. Tigg's hairbrush shows horizontal and vertical shade lines on the back.
i) The tablecloth shows no letters. There is a small number *2* below the boots.

a) The signature is similar to that in Plate A, except that the last line of the Z has been returned to the left above, instead of below the preceding line.

b) The light spot is now still darker than in Plate B.

c) The Buddha's mouth still smiles, but he wears no hat.

d) The fender shows more ornamentation.

e) Jonas' vest is plain.

f) Same as in Plate B.

g) The stem of the boot pull consists of two lines.

h) Mr. Tigg's brush shows five dots which resemble a face.

i) The tablecloth shows marks to the left of the boots which look like the letters "IN" twice repeated. Sidewise they look like a figure 2 underlined.

Mr. Nadgett breathes, as usual, an atmosphere of mystery.

Mr. Nadgett breathes, as usual, an atmosphere of mystery.

Mr. Nadgett breathes, as usual, an atmosphere of mystery.

Part XV · Plate 29 · Page 452

Mr. Pinch and Ruth Unconscious of a Visitor

This plate was etched in duplicate, the second plate numbered.

[P L A T E   A]

a) The signature is in plain capitals; the *Z* has a few flourishes, and there are two dots before the *P* and one over the *Z*.
b) There is no number on this plate unless a short horizontal line at the lower left is intended for the number 1.
c) The books on the shelves on the wall are not entirely shaded.
d) There are several lines on the paper at Tom's foot.
e) Westlock has three buttonholes in the lapel of his coat.

[P L A T E   B]

a) The signature shows more flourishes in the *Z* than it does in Plate A. There are small dots before the *P*, before the *H*, and after the *Z*.
b) There is a very small and faint *2* at the right margin, opposite the lower hem of Ruth's dress.
c) The books on the shelves are all shaded.
d) The paper near Tom's foot is blank.
e) Westlock has only two button holes in the lapel of his coat.

Mr Pinch and Ruth, unconscious of a visitor.

Mr. Pinch and Ruth, unconscious of a visitor.

Mysterious Installation of Mr. Pinch

This plate was etched in duplicate, one of them numbered.

[PLATE A]

a) The final line of the *Z* in the signature extends toward the left. The shading of the floor masks the dots, but apparently there is one above the signature and one after it, and there is a short line within the final hook of the *Z*.
b) There is no plate number.
c) There are two vertical lines over the peephole in the shutter at the left.
d) There are numerous shade lines extending downward from the right knob of the map roller.
e) The book on the chair in front of Tom is shaded horizontally.
f) The tablecloth at the right shows a pattern.
g) There are four knobs on the drawers of the center table.
h) There is a book lying flat beneath the stand at the extreme left.

[PLATE B]

a) The *Z* in the signature has no sharp angles but looks like a letter S, reversed. The lower loop is formed by the final line crossing it from above.
b) There is a very faint number below the book which extends farthest to the right. It appears like a number 1, but with a magnifying glass one can see that there is an upper dot, a line slanting from the top downward to the left, and then a wavy line forming the bottom of a *2*. It is too faint to show in the reproduction.
c) There is no line across the hole in the shutter.
d) Below the right knob of the map roller there is but a single line.
e) The book in front of Tom is shaded vertically but also with some horizontal lines crossing in the lower half.
f) The tablecloth is plain.
g) There are no knobs on the table drawers.
h) There is no book lying flat at the left of the wrapped parcel below the chair behind Westlock.

Mysterious Installation of M.ʳ Pinch.

Mysterious Installation of M.ʳ Pinch.

Mr. Jonas exhibits his presence of mind.

Part XVI · Plate 31 · Page 485

Mr. Jonas Exhibits His Presence of Mind

The plate was etched in duplicate, the second plate numbered.

[P L A T E   A]

a) The signature is plain. The upper stroke of the *Z* between a small loop and the diagonal line is missing. The final flourish returns to the left below the preceding stroke.
b) The plate is not numbered.
c) There is no tall tree extending above the lower trees in the far distance.
d) Jonas' trousers are checkered.
e) The man whose feet show over the fence is wearing spurs.
f) The bellyband of the horse in the center does not show below it.

[P L A T E   B]

a) The lower line of the *Z* in the signature forms a loop.
b) There is a small *2* at the lower right, near the base of the third fence post.
c) There is a tall tree standing out above the others in the far distance.
d) Jonas' trousers are striped.
e) There are no spurs on the upturned feet.
f) The bellyband shows under the horse's body.

Mr Jonas exhibits his presence of mind.

Part XVI · Plate 32 · Page 497

Mr. Pecksniff Announces Himself as the Shield of Virtue

This plate was etched in duplicate, neither one numbered.

[P L A T E   A]

a) The signature is simple, with a dot before the *P* and another above the *I*.
b) There are three lines in each stripe in the back of the chair in front of Mary.
c) Martin's mouth turns upward at the corner, and the rear corner of his collar does not show.
d) Six buttons are plainly visible on Mark's leggings.

[P L A T E   B]

a) There is a dot before the *P* in the signature, and the *Z* ends in a flourish.
b) There are two lines in each stripe of the chair's back.
c) Martin's mouth turns downward, and there is a point of his collar showing beneath his chin.
d) The buttons on Mark's leggings are only faintly visible.

Mr Pecksniff announces himself as the shield of Virtue.

Mr Pecksniff announces himself as the shield of Virtue.

Part XVII Plate 33 · Page 521

Mr. Moddle Is Led to the Contemplation of His Destiny

This plate was etched in duplicate, neither one definitely numbered.

[P L A T E   A]

a) The signature is plain, the *Z* ending in a straight stroke to the left. The letter *P* has an extra line, not part of the *H*, making it look like an *R*. Below Ruth's skirt there is a short vertical line that may be a figure 1.

b) Every piece of furniture and even the rug show a face which should be enough to warn customers not to marry! The poster with the lion shows only the word *Marry* in the lowest line.

c) The cloth on the bureau in the foreground shows no determinable letters.

d) The *M* of *Doohem* above the door is drawn with double lines like the other letters.

[P L A T E   B]

a) The signature has dots before and above it. The *Z* ends in a tail which looks like the figure 3. A short vertical line in the lower left corner may be a figure 1.

b) The lion poster's last line is *To Marry*. There is a vertical line below it, dividing the columns of writing.

c) The cloth on the bureau shows clearly the letters *C*, *H*, and *O*, although they may not have been intended to be letters but only ornamental lines.

d) The *M* of *Doohem* is drawn with a single line.

Mr. Moddle is led to the contemplation of his destiny.

Mr Moddle is led to the contemplation of his destiny.

Part XVII · Plate 34 · Page 528

Mrs. Gamp Makes Tea

This plate was etched in duplicate, only the second plate being numbered in very faint lines. The two plates are unusually similar, even to the lines of shading.

[PLATE A]

a) The *H* at the end of the word *Almanach* in the broadside on the wall is very clear, and there is no straight line across the tear at the left side.

b) The signature has a small circle over the *I*, and the tail of the *Z* curves upon itself from above.

c) The tea spilling from the cup at the right reaches two-thirds of the way to the woman's lap.

d) Tom's cup shows a band around it.

[PLATE B]

a) The *H* of *Almanach* is replaced by something that looks like the figure 13.

b) The signature shows the *Z* ending in a curve open to the right. There is a very faint *2* beneath the lines of the seat upon which the girl at the right is sitting.

c) The tea is spilling only about one-third of the way to the woman's knee.

d) Tom's cup does not show the ornamental band around it.

Mrs Gamp makes tea.

Mrs Gamp makes tea.

Part XVIII · Plate 35 · Page 563

Mrs. Gamp Propoges a Toast

This plate was etched in duplicate, neither plate numbered. The drawing would have been more artistic had the upper parts of the suspended dresses been omitted. They are too prominent and draw attention from the two women below.

[P L A T E   A]

a) The signature ends with a straight line to the left. There is a dot before the *P* and another over the *H*.
b) The bellows shows three nailheads on the side.
c) Nine tips of the umbrella ribs show.
d) The word *Almanac* on the one over the mantel is not clear. Numerous pins hold it up.
e) The picture frames on either side of the almanac are dark.
f) The top of the arm rest under Betsey Prig's right elbow is white.
g) There is a horizontal line defining the lower line of the panel in the door of the cupboard.

[P L A T E   B]

a) The *Z* of the signature has a loop in the tail which touches the *H* and the *I*.
b) The bellows shows no dots.
c) Only seven of the umbrella rib-tips show.
d) The word *ALMANACH* is clear, but there are no pins as fasteners.
e) The picture frames are light-colored.
f) Betsey Prig's chair arm is dark.
g) The bottom of the cupboard-door panel is not shown.

Mrs Gamp propoges a toast.

Mr. Gamp proposes a toast.

Mr. Pinch Is Amazed by an Unexpected Apparition

This plate was etched in duplicate, the second plate numbered.

[P L A T E   A]

a) "Phiz" has used an unusual signature which looks like "RHJ," but the usual dots are present before the *P* and over the *I*.

b) There is no plate number.

c) The door panel ends on a level with old Martin's right middle finger.

d) The upper portion of the latticework at the right shows some double lines.

e) The crossed lines of the wastepaper basket are single lines.

f) There are nine nails along the edge of the top shelf of the bookcase and the same number in the shelf below.

[P L A T E   B]

a) The signature resembles "PIIIZ," with a tail to the *Z* under it and ending in a loop to the right.

b) There is a large *2* below the wastepaper basket; another one, very faint in reverse, just to the left of it; and a third one, small and faint and incomplete, to the right of the basket.

c) The door panel continues downward to old Martin's left elbow.

d) The latticework is in single lines.

e) The lines of the wastepaper basket are double.

f) There are thirteen nails in the upper shelf of the bookcase and thirteen in the one below.

Mr Pinch is amazed by an unexpected apparition.   *Mr Pinch is amazed by an unexpected apparition.*

Warm Reception of Mr. Pecksniff by His Venerable Friend

This plate was etched in duplicate and probably not numbered. The titles of the falling and fallen books are very appropriate to the fallen man.

[P L A T E A]

a) The signature reads *PIIIZ*, the *Z* with elaborate flourishes. There is a dot over the *I*.

b) There is a short vertical mark in the right margin beneath Mary Graham's skirt, which may represent the figure 1. However, since Browne seldom marked the first plate when he left the second unmarked, it may be accidental.

c) There is a stopper in the bottle on the bookcase.

d) Mark Tapley's vest has vertical stripes, shown by double lines.

e) The upper edge of the upset footstool is mostly white.

[P L A T E B]

a) The signature is *PHIZ* with a dot over the *I* and one behind the *Z*.

b) The plate shows a very faint *2* to the right of the floor shading and beneath Mary's skirt. It does not show in the reproduction.

c) There is no stopper in the bottle.

d) Mark's vest is shaded by horizontal lines.

e) The upper edge of the footstool is dark.

Warm reception of Mr. Pecksniff by his venerable friend.

Plate 37 A CHUZZLEWIT / **233**

Warm reception of Mʳ Pecksniff by his venerable friends

Part XIX · Plate 38 · Page 622

The Nuptials of Miss Pecksniff Receive a Temporary Check

This plate was etched in duplicate, the second plate numbered.

[P L A T E   A]

a) The signature has dots before and after it, and there is a small circle above the *I*.
b) There is no plate number.
c) The picture of the fisherman over the door has the word *GONE* printed in reverse.
d) Charity's slippers are dark.

[P L A T E   B]

a) The signature is similar to that in Plate A. There is a dot above the *I* and possibly a small one within the upper angle of the *Z*.
b) There is a number *2* in the lower left corner.
c) The word *GONE* is now corrected.
d) Charity's slippers are now white.

The Nuptials of Miss Pecksniff receive a temporary check.

The Nuptials of Miss Pecksniff receive a temporary check.

Part XX · Plate 39 · Frontispiece

The Frontispiece was engraved in triplicate, only the third having a plate number. There are many differences between the small figures in the three plates, but only a few need be mentioned for the purpose of identification.

[PLATE A]

a) The artist's signatures on all three plates are quite similar, all being in backhand capitals. In Plate A, after a simple *Z*, the final line returns to the left and ends in a little loop with a short straight line at right angles to the base line.

b) To the left of the tau cross and above the trowel and setting maul, there are two faces.

c) The kneeling Pecksniff at the bottom of the plate has a white vest and shirt.

d) The moneybag in the hands of the figure in the same group whose abdomen is marked with a face carries the figures *0001*.

e) The figure above the teapot and below the dragon at the left center of the plate is very faintly marked with letters which look like "Pisc" but were probably intended for "Prig."

f) At the upper left, between the houses and the marginal musical notes and birdcage, there is an almost straight line of figures which appear in all three plates with but slight variations. A man with his right arm akimbo projects a little beyond the main line. In Plate A there are no other figures to the left of him.

g) The bag in front of the prostrate Jonas and at the feet of the shrouded figure above the large tripod and the moon is marked *0001*.

h) Between the owl and the pussycat at the right of the center there is a branch with leaves.

i) The crossbar of the chair in which Tom Pinch's sister is sitting, as well as the adjacent parts, is only faintly sketched.

[PLATE B]

a) The final stroke of the flourish below the signature ends in a double loop at the left. There are dots above and after the name.

b) To the left of the tau cross there are seven more or less rudimentary faces.

c) Pecksniff at the bottom of the picture has a shaded vest but a white shirt.

d) The moneybag in the same group is marked *1001*.

e) The figure above the teapot and below the dragon is plainly marked *Prig*.

f) There are musical notes and three additional figures to the left of the man with his arm akimbo.

g) The bag in front of the prostrate Jonas is marked *0001*.

h) Between the owl and the pussycat nothing appears along the window frame.

i) The crossbar shows distinctly in Tom Pinch's sister's chair.

[PLATE C]

a) The signature ends with a flourish and a loop to the right. After the signature there is a dot and the figure *3* reversed.

b) There are no faces to the left of the tau cross.

c) Pecksniff has a shaded vest and shirt.

d) The moneybag is rather indistinctly marked *100*.

e) The figure above the teapot is not marked.

f) The small musical notes do not appear, but there are three men and a woman with a child in her arms to the left of the man with his arm akimbo.

g) The bag in front of Jonas is marked *1000*.

h) Between the owl and the pussycat there are some leaves and a handle to the window.

i) There are vertical spindles in the back of Ruth Pinch's chair.

The title-page was etched in triplicate, probably none numbered, although it is easy to see, in the lines of the foliage, grass, or the shading of the foreground, curves which may be interpreted as a figure 2 or 3. The publishers' imprint at the bottom of the page is London/Chapman and Hall/MDCCCXLIV. The first C in the date is interlocked with the second, which is almost a complete circle.

[PLATE A]

a) The sign on the post is marked *100£*, and, while it was once thought that this indicated the earliest etching, it is not now so regarded, since all three plates were printed at the same time. It was probably the first plate engraved, however, for the signature, followed by *fecit*, had not been used by Browne since he signed the Frontispiece of *Pickwick*.

b) The signature is in capital letters, with the *Z* reversed and a dot over the *I*. It is followed by *fecit*.

c) Seven rivets are shown in the lid of the trunk standing on the ground.

d) The tire of the left wheel of the one-hoss shay (that is, the tire to the right in the etching) shows two rivets above the joint.

[PLATE B]

a) The signpost is clearly marked £100.

b) The reversed *Z* in the signature has long top and bottom lines. There is a small circle over it.

c) There are five rivets in the lid of the trunk.

d) The tire shows no rivets either above or below the joint.

[PLATE C]

a) The signpost is marked £100, but not so clearly as in Plate B.

b) The signature is in capitals, with the *Z* reversed and with loops at the top and bottom. A reversed *3* may be only grass.

c) Six rivets show in the lid of the trunk.

d) The tire shows one rivet above and one below the joint.

MARTIN CHUZZLEWIT

BY

CHARLES DICKENS

LONDON

CHAPMAN AND HALL.

MDCCCXLIV.

Dealings
with the Firm of

DOMBEY AND SON

Martin Chuzzlewit ended in July, 1844, and was followed in January, 1846, by *Oliver Twist* in ten monthly parts. This, however, was a reprint of a story which originally appeared as a serial in *Bentley's Miscellany* between February, 1837, and March, 1839. It does not come into consideration in this book because the illustrations were by George Cruikshank and not by Hablôt K. Browne.

Dickens' next book was *Dombey and Son*. This, as usual, was issued in twenty monthly parts, bound in nineteen, between October, 1846, and April, 1848. Counting the Frontispiece and title-page, there were 40 plates, all of them etched in duplicate, making a total of 80 steels. Because these proved insufficient to supply the demand, lithographs were made of many of them, perhaps of all. Usually these can be distinguished from the etchings by a heavier appearance, both of the drawings and of the legends, and often by the blocking of the shadows. Eckel said that the lithographs were made later than the etchings, while Hatton and Cleaver said that they were used simultaneously and that even copies in the parts show mixtures of the two. It has generally been thought that no lithographs were issued before they appeared in *Dombey*, but to me some of the plates in *Martin Chuzzlewit* look suspiciously like lithographs.

Until the appearance of the twentieth plate in *Dombey*, all the illustrations were upright on the page, but, beginning with that plate, some were made with the horizon parallel to the long edge of the book. Five were thus made for *Dombey*, and later 21 for *Copperfield*, 19 for *Bleak House*, 27 for *Little Dorrit*, and 14 for *A Tale of Two Cities*. Also in *Dombey* appeared for the first time etchings that have come to be called the "dark plates," which are a combination of machine ruling (engraving) and etching, producing a nice effect of light and shade, especially for night scenes. Plate 35 was the first and only one of these in *Dombey*. The next appeared as Plate 31 of *David Copperfield*.

In the interval between the ending of *Martin Chuzzlewit* in July, 1844, and the beginning of *Dombey and Son*, October, 1846, Browne produced over 77 woodcuts, including 68 for Rodwell's *Memoirs of an Umbrella*, and a few etchings, including 26 for Lever's *The O'Donoghue*. While *Dombey and Son* was being issued, he etched, besides the 80 steels for that work, 20 for Carleton's *Valentine McClutchy*, 40 for Lever's *Knight of Gwynne*, 22 for LeFanu's *Torlogy O'Brien*, 2 for Ainsworth's *Old Saint Paul's*, and a few of less importance.

Miss Tox introduces "the Party"

Part I · Plate 1 · Page 10

Miss Tox Introduces "the Party"

[P L A T E A]

a) There is no number on this plate unless the final straight line of the tail of the *Z* is intended for one.
b) In the legend there is no upstroke at the beginning of the *i* of *introduces*.
c) The child at the left has no stick in her hand.
d) The taller of the two boys has three buttons on his vest.

[P L A T E B]

a) The number *2* follows the signature, and three dots precede it.
b) There is an upstroke at the beginning of the letter *i* of the word *introduces*.
c) The child at the left has a stick in her hand.
d) The taller boy has five buttons on his vest.

Miss Tox introduces "the Party"

Part I · Plate 2 · Page 22

The Dombey Family

The earlier etchings for Dickens' novels were marred by heavy shading at the tops. This is entirely absent in the *Dombey* plates, even in such plates as this, which previously would have been made very dark above the chandelier.

[PLATE A]

a) There is a wavy line below Florence's skirt, resembling a figure 2, and if it were not for the fact that there is a similar zigzag line in the same position in the other plate, I should consider it the plate number. The right-angled drop in the flourish below the signature may have been intended for the figure 1.
b) There is a short dash in the top margin of the newspaper at Dombey's feet, representing the masthead.
c) The bottom line of the lower door panel is shown.
d) There is nothing on the shelf below the mirror.
e) There is nothing in the baby's left hand.
f) The picture on the wall at the left clearly shows a ship.

[PLATE B]

a) The end of the flourish below the signature is a wavy line.
b) There is nothing at the top of the newspaper.
c) The bottom line of the door panel is not shown.
d) There is a vase at each end of the shelf below the mirror.
e) The baby has a rattle in its left hand.
f) The picture at the left shows a woman standing on a dock or something. There is no ship in sight.

The Dombey Family

The Dombey Family.

Part II · Plate 3 · Page 40

The Christening Party

A scratchy etching in which Mr. Dombey appears in his favorite character of a stuffed shirt.

[P L A T E   A]

a) There is no plate number.
b) The map on the wall in front of Dombey shows no suspension cord.
c) Dombey's back hair shows in the mirror. His watch has only one good hand and a fragment of another.
d) The collar of the woman with the flower garden on her hat is shown by shade lines.

[P L A T E   B]

a) A *2* follows the signature.
b) The map on the wall shows the cord by which it is suspended.
c) Dombey's watch shows two hands. His reflection in the mirror does not show his back hair.
d) The dress of the woman with the floral hat shows no collar.

The Christening Party.

The Christening Party.

Polly Rescues the Charitable Grinder

One of Browne's strong points was his rendering of mob scenes, especially the less distinct appearance of the distant parts.

[PLATE A]

a) The plate has no number, unless the tail end of the signature represents a figure 1.

b) There are three and a half awnings over the windows shown in front of the coachman.

c) The footman on the coach wears two epaulets.

d) The coachman has a button on his left sleeve.

e) The number on the shoulder of the Charitable Grinder is *147*, but each figure is reversed.

f) The woman bending over the fallen woman at the right center does not have shade lines over her entire dress.

[PLATE B]

a) There is a *2* after the signature *PHIZ*.

b) There are four and a half awnings shown.

c) The footman has only one epaulet.

d) The coachman has no button on his left sleeve.

e) The number on the boy's shoulder is not reversed.

f) The woman bending over the woman who has fallen to the ground in the right center has shade lines over her entire dress.

Polly rescues the Charitable Grinder.

Polly rescues the Charitable Grinder.

Part III · Plate 5 · Page 75

Paul and Mrs. Pipchin

Dickens' comment on this illustration has been preserved in a letter to John Forster, November, 1846, and reprinted in Walter Dexter's *Letters of Charles Dickens*. He said:

I was really *distressed* by the illustration of Mrs. Pipchin and Paul. It is so frightfully and widely wide of the mark. Good Heaven! in the commonest and most literal construction of the text, it is all wrong. She is described as an old lady, and Paul's "miniature arm-chair" is mentioned more than once. He ought to be sitting in a little arm-chair down in the corner of the fireplace, staring up at her. I can't say what pain and vexation it is to be so utterly misrepresented. I would cheerfully have given a hundred pounds to have kept this illustration out of the book. He never could have got that idea of Mrs. Pipchin if he had attended to the text. Indeed I think he does better without the text; for then the notion is made easy to him in short description, and he can't help taking it in.

After all, the plate is not too bad, and Dickens was troubling himself about something that relatively few readers would notice.

[P L A T E   A]

a) The tail of the flourish in the signature ends at the left in a right angle, finishing with a line that may possibly be intended for a number 1.
b) The vines in the flowerpots above Paul's head and in the center of the room are without thorns.
c) Back of the cactus plant at the right, there is no window box.
d) The bits of the keys in the basket on the table are white.
e) The orifice of the bellows is more or less egg-shaped.
f) There are vertical lines of pleats in Paul's waist.
g) There is an ornament on the back of Mrs. Pipchin's chair at the meeting of the middle rail with the toppiece.

Paul and Mrs. Pipchin

Paul and Mrs Pipch..

a) The signature ends in a loop, then a curve and a horizontal line.
b) The vines hanging from the flowerpots are thorny.
c) A window box with a flowerpot appears back of the cactus on the table.
d) The bits of the keys in the basket are dark.
e) The orifice in the bellows is rectangular.
f) There are no pleats in Paul's waist.
g) The ornament in Mrs. Pipchin's chair is in the center of the toppiece.

Part III · Plate 6 · Page 87

Captain Cuttle Consoles His Friend

[P L A T E   A]

a) There is a dot before the signature and a small circle above it. It is followed by a short, straight mark which may have been intended for the
figure 1.
b) No hands appear on the watch in front of Captain Cuttle. His vest shows
four buttons on the wrong side of the overlap, and one end of his cravat
touches his coat lapel at his right.
c) There is a drawstring at the left of the door curtain.
d) The alidade of the sextant at the extreme right is unshaded.

[P L A T E   B]

a) The signature is followed by a mark like the English pound sign, but without the crossed bar, and may have been intended for the figure 2.
b) The watch has hands. Captain Cuttle's vest has six buttons. Neither end
of his cravat touches his coat lapel.
c) There is no drawstring to the door curtain.
d) The alidade is shaded.

Captain Cuttle consoles his Friend.

Captain Cuttle consoles his Friend.

Part IV · Plate 7 · Page 113

Doctor Blimber's Young Gentlemen as They Appeared
when Enjoying Themselves

Most of the "young gentlemen" show by their expressions
their envy of the freedom of the town boys. "The doctor only
takes ten young gentlemen," says the text; the drawing shows
sixteen, exclusive of Paul.

[P L A T E   A]

a) The heels of the shoes of the boy performing on the guardrail show no
iron inlays.
b) In the background at the right, the man on the mule wears a pointed nightcap.
c) The boy's kite has shade lines across it.
d) The Bath chairs on the beach are carelessly drawn and may as well represent rocks.

[P L A T E   B]

a) The heels of the boy gymnast show horseshoe insets.
b) The man on the mule wears a round cap.
c) The kite has a face but no cross-shading.
d) The Bath chairs are clearly shown, including their wheels.

*Doctor Blimber's Young Gentlemen as
they appeared when enjoying themselves.*

Doctor Blimber's Young Gentlemen as they appeared when enjoying themselves.

Paul's Exercises

Florence's way of helping Paul is of more help to her than to Paul.

[PLATE A]

a) The portrait over the mantel is suspended by a cord.
b) Susan Nipper's chair back shows horizontal lines across the central uprights.
c) Only one table leg shows.
d) Florence's chair back has an ornament in the top crosspiece. The bow in front of the collar of her dress is dark but is not easily recognized as a bow.
e) The handle of the flat candlestick is not circular.

[PLATE B]

a) The portrait over the mantel shows no cord.
b) Susan's chair back shows three distinct uprights besides the side rail, but no horizontal lines across them.
c) Two table legs show.
d) Florence's chair back has no ornament at the top. The bow on her dress is quite distinct.
e) The candlestick has a circular handle.

Pauls exercises.

Pauls exercise.

Part V · Plate 9 · Page 145

Paul Goes Home for the Holidays

It is not necessary to read the text to see how well Paul was liked by his schoolmates, even by the "young gentlemen" and the instructors. It is also easy to see why the maid in the archway was well liked by the boys. Florence is unusually good looking for a "Phiz" young woman, and the older boys clearly show their approval of her.

[PLATE A]

a) The plain signature has a small vertical line within the *Z* and another after it, the latter probably intended for the number 1, since it occupies a position close to that of the number in Plate B.

b) The thumb of the good-natured maid up the stairway does not show, and her apron is not heavily shaded.

c) The butler does not wear a stickpin in his cravat.

d) The boy to the right of Florence has no shirt studs, and the young gentleman to the right of him wears a single flower on his coat lapel.

e) The footman to the right of the butler has three buttons on his coat.

[PLATE B]

a) Below the signature there are two small vertical lines which may represent the number 2.

b) The good-natured maid's thumb shows, and her apron is quite dark.

c) The butler has a stickpin in his cravat.

d) The boy to the right of Florence has two shirt studs, and the kinky-haired, balding gentleman at his left shows two blossoms in his coat lapel.

e) The footman has four buttons on his coat.

Paul goes home for the holidays.

Paul goes home for the holidays

Profound Cogitation of Captain Cuttle

[P L A T E   A]

a) The signature ends in a straight line to the left with a dot below the end.
b) The top shelf of the china closet shows three goblets.
c) The lowest shelf has a decanter and two jugs(?).
d) The door shows a keyhole but no escutcheon plate.
e) The left upper corner of the mantel is plain except for shading.

[P L A T E   B]

a) The signature ends at the left in a sharp angle, and the line returns to the right, then in a curve again to the left. There are dots before the *P*, before the uncrossed *H*, and after the *Z*.
b) The top shelf has four goblets.
c) The lowest shelf shows two decanters.
d) The keyhole shows an escutcheon plate.
e) The upper corner of the mantel shows a circle.

Profound cogitation of Captain Cuttle.

Profound cogitation of Captain Cuttle.

Part VI · Plate 11 · Page 179

Poor Paul's Friend

[P L A T E   A]

a) The signature is partly covered by the shading of the floor.
b) A book leans to the left near the left end of the second shelf from the top.
c) The cover of the book on the floor nearest the lower left corner is shaded.
d) The book under Florence's elbow is shaded with diagonal lines.
e) The links of the chain on the floor are shown by double lines.
f) The thread between the ball of yarn on the floor and the table leg is indicated by a single line.

[P L A T E   B]

a) The signature is entirely within the shading of the floor and is hardly legible.
b) All the books on the second shelf from the top are upright.
c) The book on the floor at the lower left has a white cover with some markings which are partly ornaments, but one line makes a very good figure *2.*
d) The book under Florence's elbow has diagonal shade lines as well as lines representing printing.
e) The links of the chain are shown by single lines.
f) The thread between the ball and the table leg is shown by a double line. The ball is no longer in the white space of the floor but has replaced the flower shown in Plate A.

Poor Paul's Friend

Poor Paul's Friend

Part VI · Plate 12 · Page 185

The Wooden Midshipman on the Lookout

The wooden midshipman's hands are held in positions suggestive of those of Mark Twain's petrified Indian.

[P L A T E   A]

a) There is a space between the wooden midshipman's ankles.
b) The poster in the lower left corner clearly shows the word *Calcutta*.
c) The ends of the trunk on the cart and the one below it have no nailheads.
d) Above the show window are the words *SHIP'S INSTRU* . . . , the letters after the *U* fading out.
e) Below the word *OUTFIT* on the sign at the top center is the word *WORLD*. The panel below is clearly drawn.

[P L A T E   B]

a) The wooden midshipman's ankles show no space between them.
b) The first four letters of *Calcutta* on the poster are all that are determinable.
c) The end of the trunk on the cart shows two nailheads, and the one being lifted by the man shows five.
d) There is no lettering over the show window.
e) Below the word *OUTFIT* there is only an ornamental scroll.

The Wooden Midshipman on the look out.

The Wooden Midshipman on the look out.

Part VII · Plate 13 · Page 204

Major Bagstock Is Delighted To Have That Opportunity

An excellent drawing except for the excessive caricaturing of Major Bagstock and the Native.

[P L A T E   A]

a) The signature has a fancy *Z*, whose lower line, after a slight break, turns downward at right angles, possibly representing the figure 1. There is a dot before and another above the word *PHIZ*.

b) The first *t* of the word *that* in the legend begins with an upstroke.

c) The sign on the hotel is written backward, and there is a crossline connecting the tops of the two verticals of the letter *H*.

d) The tassel hanging from the tip of Edith Skewton Granger's parasol is very faintly shown.

e) The veil of the lady on horseback at the left is unshaded.

[P L A T E   B]

a) The signature lies in the shaded ground and has little ornamentation.

b) The first *t* of the word *that* in the legend begins at the top.

c) There is no line connecting the tops of the two verticals of the letter *H* in *Hotel*, but the word is still reversed.

d) The tassel on Mrs. Granger's parasol is dark.

e) The veil of the lady on horseback is crossed by horizontal lines.

Major Bagstock is delighted to have that opportunity

Part VII · Plate 14 · Page 223

Mr. Toots Becomes Particular—Diogenes Also

[P L A T E   A]

a) The signature in the lower right corner shows few flourishes. The *Z* ends in a straight line to the left, and there is a dot before the *P*.
b) Mr. Toots's cane is rather dark.
c) The inner vertical lines of the wall panel are double.
d) There is a tassel attached to the cane in the stand at the extreme left.
e) In the legend, the *p* of *particular* begins with a downstroke.
f) The clock face is shaded by vertical lines.

[P L A T E   B]

a) The signature ends in a flourish at the left, and there are dots above and after the name.
b) Mr. Toots's cane is defined by two thin lines.
c) The vertical lines and part of the upper horizontal line of the wall panel are single.
d) There is no tassel on the cane in the umbrella rack.
e) There is an upstroke at the beginning of the *p* of *particular*.
f) The clock face is shaded by vertical and diagonal lines.

Mr. Toots becomes particular — Diogenes also.

Mr. Toots becomes particular — Diogenes also.

Part VIII · Plate 15 · Page 238

Solemn Reference Is Made to Mr. Bunsby

[PLATE A]

a) The signature in plain capitals lacks the cross-stroke of the *H* and consequently looks like "PIIIZ." The *Z* ends in an acute angle at the left. A dot precedes the *P*, and there is a figure *1* below the *Z*.

b) Only a small dot indicates the hand of the clock at the right.

c) The back of the chair behind Captain Cuttle shows decorations which look like Chinese characters.

d) In the picture on the wall in the center, the persons in the small boat leaving the wreck are not recognizable as people.

[PLATE B]

a) The signature ends in a loop at the left, and there is a small circle after the *Z*. A wavy line above the name may be a reversed *2*.

b) The hands of the clock point to three o'clock.

c) The decorations on the back of Captain Cuttle's chair are **S**-shaped.

d) The small boat in the picture shows approximately five persons in it.

Solemn reference is made to Mr. Bunsby.

Solemn reference is made to Mr. Bunsby

**Mr. Carker Introduces Himself to Florence
and the Skettles Family**

Does a mounted horse ever stand with two feet off the
ground?

[P L A T E   A]

a) The house in the cental background shows a belfry with a square opening,
   within which there are several crossed lines. The side of the house shows
   three windows in the second story.
b) Inclosed in the pediment of this house are two triangles and a central circle.
   The windows below have rectangular lintels.
c) The house to the left has a bell in the belfry and a clock whose hands point
   to approximately the hour of four.
d) There is no handkerchief showing in Mr. Carker's top coat pocket.

[P L A T E   B]

a) The central belfry has an arched top and a bell within. The house has
   only two windows at the right of the central portion.
b) The pediment shows two sloping lines and a central horseshoe-shaped
   ornament. The windows have curved lines above them.
c) The house to the left has only vertical shade lines in the belfry. The clock
   is shaded.
d) Carker's handkerchief shows in his upper coat pocket.

Mr Carker introduces himself to Florence & the Skettle family.

Mr Carker introduces himself to Florence & the Skettle family.

Joe B is sly Sir, devilish sly

Part IX · Plate 17 · Page 267

Joe B Is Sly, Sir, Devilish Sly

[P L A T E   A]

a) The signature *PIIIZ* ends in a curve returning to the right.

b) There are numerous scratches below the feet of the Native but no number. There is, however, a short vertical mark in the margin at the right opposite the Native's calves, which may perhaps be intended for a Roman numeral I.

c) The picture on the wall is not very plainly marked *TOBY.W.WAL.*, and the girl's left hand rests in her lap.

d) The second candle from the left shows two rays extending downward.

[P L A T E   B]

a) There is a dot in front of the signature *RIIZ*, which ends in a straight line to the left.

b) Beneath the feet of the Native are two short horizontal lines which may indicate Plate 2, but it is doubtful.

c) In the picture on the wall, which is plainly marked *TOBY WAD*, the girl's left hand touches her chin.

d) The second candle shows no beams emanating from it.

Joe B is sly Sir; devilish sly.

Part IX · Plate 18 · Page 288

Mr. Dombey Introduces His Daughter Florence

"Phiz" was uncommonly successful in making Edith a pretty woman, but Florence's face is unattractive, as are most of "Phiz's" women. Mr. Dombey as a newly married man is good.

[P L A T E   A]

a) The signature ends in a straight line to the left. The *H* has no crossbar; there is a short, straight line before the name and a dot above the *H* and after the *Z*.
b) Above Dombey's head there is a short, straight line that may be interpreted as a figure 1.
c) The whitewash bucket on the stepladder has a bail handle.
d) The handles of the two paintbrushes in the foreground cross.
e) The top picture frame back of the new Mrs. Dombey is without shade lines.

[P L A T E   B]

a) The signature ends in a flourish at the left. The *H* is like that in Plate A, but there are no dots.
b) Above Dombey's head is a distinct figure 2, which may be intended for the number of the plate, since the preceding one shows the figure *1* in the same place.
c) There is no bail on the bucket.
d) The handles of the paintbrushes touch but do not cross.
e) The top picture back of Mrs. Dombey shows vertical shade lines.

Mr Dombey introduces his daughter Florence.

Mr Dombey introduces his daughter Florence.

Part X · Plate 19 · Page 294

The Eyes of Mrs. Chick Are Opened to Lucretia Tox

[P L A T E   A]

a) The signature is preceded by a small circle and extends in a waved line to the left.
b) The cupid on the cabinet at the right is lightly shaded over his left ear.
c) The folio at the right is without a title, and the cabinet below has diagonal lines across the horizontal shading of the front.
d) Miss Tox's left sole is unshaded.
e) An earring shows in the Native's left ear.
f) In the legend, the *x* of *Tox* is without a flourish at the end.

[P L A T E   B]

a) The signature has curlicues both before and after it, and there is no cross-bar to the letter *H*.
b) The cupid seems to be wearing a hearing aid.
c) The folio is marked *ALBUM* within an oval, and the cabinet below has diagonal lines both ways.
d) Miss Tox's sole is shaded.
e) No earring shows in the Native's ear.
f) The *x* of *Tox* in the legend ends in a loop.

The eyes of M.ͬˢ Chick are opened to Lucretia Tox

The eyes of Mrs Chick are opened to Lucretia Tox

Part X · Plate 20 · Page 316

Coming Home from Church

This is the first of the "horizontal plates," of which 5 appeared in *Dombey*, 21 in *David Copperfield*, 19 in *Bleak House*, 27 in *Little Dorrit*, and 14 in *A Tale of Two Cities*. The latter are not shown in this book, for they do not occur in duplicate. The backgrounds of both plates seem to be machine-ruled in two directions in various places. Neither is numbered.

In spite of the great amount of detail in this plate, it is highly successful. "Phiz's" ability as an artist is shown by his reproduction of the natural lack of resemblance between the faces of the various individuals and as an etcher by the relief between foreground and background.

[P L A T E   A]

a) The artist's signature ends in a sharp point at the left and a short return to the right. Below this at right angles is a short line, which may be intended for the figure 1. There is a dot above the *I* and a short detached curve after the *Z*.
b) At the top of the building at the upper right there are four windows.
c) The man with his finger to his nose at the left of the Punch and Judy show has a patch on the back of his coat.
d) There is no loop at the end of the word *Church* in the legend.

[P L A T E   B]

a) The signature ends in a loop at the left, and there is a broken circle after it.
b) The are sketchy indications of six or seven windows at the upper right.
c) The man at the left of the Punch and Judy show has no patch on the back of his coat.
d) There is a loop after the *h* in the word *Church* in the legend.

Coming home from Church.

Coming home from Church

Part XI · Plate 21 · Page 325

A Visitor of Distinction

The wooden midshipman is more respectful indoors than out.

[P L A T E   A]

a) The signature has a figure *1* below the letter *Z*.
b) The telescope in front of the desk does not show the crossline of a sunshade, and the chronometer near it has no hands.
c) The chest at the lower left shows no handle.
d) The desk on which Rob the Grinder is leaning has a single broad panel at the end.

[P L A T E   B]

a) The signature ends at the left in a large flourish.
b) The telescope in front of the desk shows distinctly the top line of the sunshade. The chronometer shows its hands.
c) The chest at the lower left has a handle.
d) The desk shows two panels at the end.

A Visitor of distinction.

A Visitor of distinction

Part XI · Plate 22 · Page 352

The Rejected Alms

[PLATE A]

a) The signature ends in a line to the left, with a very small curl at the end.
b) The three coins immediately in front of the step lie nearly in a straight line.
c) There are three coins falling from Alice Marwood's hand.
d) The front of Alice's left ankle is unshaded.
e) In the legend the *r* of *rejected* begins below the base line.

[PLATE B]

a) The signature has a large curved line in front of it.
b) The three coins in front of the step form the corners of a triangle.
c) There are only two coins falling from Alice's hand.
d) Alice's left ankle is almost entirely shaded by vertical lines.
e) The *r* of *rejected* in the legend does not extend below the base line.

The rejected alms.

The rejected alms.

Mrs. Dombey at Home

As usual, this drawing is like the perfect setting of a stage. In spite of the many figures, it gives the impression of a crowd without being crowded. This is the second horizontal plate.

[P L A T E A]

a) The signature is quite fancy, with a dot before it and one above the *I*. The lower line of the *Z* ends in a loop at the left.
b) The top lines of the door casing are three in number.
c) The candles to the left of the door are represented by four lines for those at the left of the mirror and five for those at the right.
d) The coat of the tall man with his two index fingers joined is shaded.
e) At the right margin, the shade lines of the door opening extend downward as far as the Jewish woman's waist.

[P L A T E B]

a) The signature ends at the left in a straight line. There are dots within the *Z* and after the signature. Very faint marks to the left of the signature seem to be another signature in small backhand capitals, probably nearly burnished out. There is no indication of a number unless short vertical lines below the top and below the center of the table represent the figure 1. It is doubtful.
b) There are only two lines at the top of the door casing at the right.
c) The candles at the left of the door, which stands open, are represented by three lines at each side of the mirror.
d) The coat of the tall man is entirely unshaded.
e) The shading of the door opening ends above the head of the woman.

Mrs Dombey at Home.

Mrs Dombey at Home.

Part XII · Plate 24 · Page 381

Miss Tox Pays a Visit to the Toodle Family

[P L A T E A]

a) The signature, *PIHZ*, has a dot before it and one above the *I*.
b) There are four plates on the next to the top shelf behind the door.
c) The wheels of the locomotive on the floor show no hubs.
d) Miss Tox's shoe is shaded.

[P L A T E B]

a) The signature ends in a straight line to the left.
b) There are five plates on the shelf.
c) The wheels of the locomotive show distinct hubs.
d) Miss Tox's shoe is white.

Miss Tox pays a visit to the Toodle Family.

Miss Tox pays a visit to the Toodle Family

The Midshipman Is Boarded by the Enemy

[PLATE A]

a) The *Z* of the signature ends in a line to the left, which turns down at a sharp angle to form a straight line below, possibly intended for a 1.
b) The picture on the wall at the left is labeled *Medusa*.
c) The face of the banjo clock is shaded.
d) The door at the left shows a keyhole. A single line forms the top of the lower door panel.
e) Bunsby's handkerchief shows as an almost circular white spot above his coat pocket.
f) The *i* of *is* in the legend begins with an upstroke.

[PLATE B]

a) The signature ends in a loop at the left. There is a dot above the *H*, and the *Z* is reversed.
b) There is no name under the picture of the ship.
c) The banjo clock shows no shading on the face, but the hands show four o'clock.
d) The door at the left has no keyhole, only a little dot at the left and a small circle at the right of the knob. The top of the lower door panel is formed by two lines.
e) Bunsby's handkerchief is shaded and is of irregular shape.
f) The letter *i* of *is* in the legend begins at the top.

The Midshipman is boarded by the enemy.

The Midshipman is boarded by the enemy.

Part XIII · Plate 26 · Page 408

A Chance Meeting

This is the third horizontal plate. According to the size of the figures in the foreground, Edith and Alice must have been seven feet tall.

$$[\,\text{P L A T E} \quad \text{A}\,]$$

a) The signature ends with a letter *Z* that looks like a script 3. There is one dot in front of the *Z* and one within it.
b) The coach lamp is poorly defined.
c) The footman's hat does not show a white band.
d) There are two reins from the horses to the coachman's hands.

$$[\,\text{P L A T E} \quad \text{B}\,]$$

a) The last letter of the signature ends in a curve open to the left. Four dots are shown—before, behind, above, and below the name.
b) The coach lamp is clearly shown.
c) The footman's hat shows a definite white band.
d) There are three reins from the horses to the coachman's hands.

A chance Meeting.

A chance Meeting.

Part XIV · Plate 27 · Page 424

Mr. Dombey and His "Confidential Agent"

[P L A T E   A]

a) The signature is crowded, and the *Z* is drawn across the other letters. There is a dot in front of the *P* and a flourish forming a double loop under the whole name, finally ending in a line to the right.

b) There are no shade lines on top of the footstool, only the lines of the ornamentation.

c) The confidential agent's trousers show stripes, and he has three buttons in his shirt front.

d) No buttons show in Dombey's shirt.

e) The carving knife and fork in the roast at the left are sketchy.

f) A line of dots crosses the leg of the nude girl in the picture on the wall.

[P L A T E   B]

a) The signature is more open, the *Z* ends in a flourish to the right, and there is a curved line, resembling the figure 2, in front.

b) The top of the footstool is shaded.

c) The agent's trousers are plain, and there are no buttons in his shirt front.

d) One rudimentary button is shown in Dombey's shirt.

e) The carving knife and fork in the roast at the left are clearly drawn.

f) The girl's leg is free from spots.

Mr. Dombey and his "confidential agent".

Mr. Dombey and his "confidential agent"

Florence Parts from a Very Old Friend

And now Mrs. Pipchin is at least seven feet tall.

[P L A T E   A]

a) The lower line of the Z of the signature ends at the left in a right angle downward, and there is another short line, which may represent the figure 1, to the left of it.

b) The keys in Mrs. Pipchin's hand have dark bits.

c) There is no cord around the trunk in the footman's hands except the diagonal one that he is holding.

d) The letters *f* in the legend end on the downstrokes of the main stems.

[P L A T E   B]

a) The tail end of the Z in the signature ends at the left in a little circle.

b) The keys in Mrs. Pipchin's hand have light-colored bits.

c) There is a cord running across the lid of the trunk.

d) The letters *f* of the legend are carried upward from the lowest ends and join the letters *r* following.

Florence parts from a very old friend

Florence parts from a very old friend.

Part XV · Plate 29 · Page 450

Abstraction and Recognition

[PLATE A]

a) The signature is in capital letters, with the final flourish of the *Z* ending in a straight line to the left. There are dots before, above, and after the signature.

b) In the legend the crossing of the lines in the tail of the letter *g* is over one-third the way down.

c) The straps from the curb bit of Mr. Carker's horse are single lines. The handle of his whip touches his whiskers.

d) Beginning at the archway, the posters read: *To those about to marry* (the *S* of *those* reversed); *Theatre, City Madam* (in two lines); *Cruikshank bottle* (with a picture of a bottle and the *S* of *Cruikshank* reversed and with the left half of the poster heavily shaded). In the next vertical row there are three posters, the central one with the word *Moses* (the *S* reversed) and the others blank. The final poster at the right is marked *Lull . . . Bal Masque* (with the *S* of the last word reversed).

[PLATE B]

a) The last line of the *Z* in the signature ends at the left in a sharp angle and a return line curved downward to the right.

b) In the legend the final line of the *g* crosses near the base line.

c) The straps of the curb bit are shown as double lines. There is a white space between the handle of Mr. Carker's whip and his face.

d) Beginning at the archway, the posters read: *To thos. . . . Marry* (the *S* of *those* correct); *Theatre . . . City Mad . . .* (in three lines). In the next column of posters there are three with lettering instead of one: *Observe; Cruicshank Bottle-* (with a picture of a bottle as before and the name "Cruikshank" spelled with a *c*); and *Down Again 6* (in three lines). In the next to the last row of posters there are now four instead of three, all show signs of lettering, but only the *Moses* one is clear. The final poster at the right seems to read "JULIICU BAL."

Abstraction & Recognition

Abstraction & Recognition

Part XV · Plate 30 · Page 469

Florence and Edith on the Staircase

The scrollwork in the stair railing is quite different in the two plates, but the variation is difficult to describe in words.

[PLATE A]

a) The signature ends with a line to the left. There are dots before and after the signature and over the *I*.

b) The wall panel at Edith's right elbow shows a single line at the top and below it three horizontal lines.

c) In the top painting at the left, the diagonal shade lines do not cover the owl or "little Eva and the angel" except the latter's wing. In the panel to the right of this, the diagonal shade lines do not cover the angel's face.

d) The young lady from Niger who went for a ride on a tiger—though the tiger looks more like a bear—in the glass case on the stairway landing has no shading on her knee.

e) Venus at the right shows a roll of hair across her forehead. The hair is parted, and there is a flower at the left.

[PLATE B]

a) The extension of the *Z* in the signature ends at the left in a curve like the figure 2. There are dots before, above, and after the name.

b) The wall panel at Edith's elbow shows only two horizontal lines below the top line.

c) Diagonal shade lines cover the owl, the angel, and the baby. In the matching panel to the right of this, the diagonal lines shade the angel's face.

d) There are shade lines on the knee of the lady on the tiger.

e) Venus' hair shows no parting, no roll across the front, and no flower.

Florence & Edith on the Staircase

Florence & Edith on the Staircase

290 / DOMBEY *Plates 30A and 30B*

The Shadow in the Little Parlor

In the text the word "parlor" is spelled "parlour" by Dickens, but in the legend it has the American form "parlor." Cf. Plate 25, of the *Pickwick Papers*.

The text says that it was twilight outside, and "the light of the fire was shining on the walls and ceiling of the little room." The shadow upon the wall, therefore, is incorrectly placed, for it is where Captain Cuttle's shadow should fall. It should not be that of Walter Gay, for he was behind Florence, for Dickens says she "started up, looked round, and . . . saw Walter Gay behind her." Perhaps there was a convenient street light outside to throw the shadow where it fell! In that case, that portion of the shadow on the door should have been omitted.

[PLATE A]

a) The signatures on the two plates are very similar. There are, however, two dots and a vertical line, which may be a figure 1, some distance below the signature in Plate A.

b) There is a fire tong but no poker on the fender.

c) Below the point where Captain Cuttle's toasting fork penetrates the toast, there are no dots.

d) There is no point of suspension above the oval picture at the upper left. It shows diagonal shading in the boy's coat. The boat in the center picture clearly shows a bowsprit and two masts.

e) There is a doorknob but nothing else near the edge of the door, **and** there is nothing except shading along the edge itself.

f) The leg of the seat at the lower right shows a knob at the lower end, **and** there is **a** small circle at the top.

The Shadow in the little parlor.

The Shadow in the little parlor.

a) There are neither dots nor a vertical line beneath the signature.

b) There are fire tongs as well as a poker on the fender.

c) There are two very short vertical lines or two spots beneath the point of Captain Cuttle's hook.

d) The coat of the boy in the oval frame is shaded by vertical lines, and there is a hanger above the frame.

e) There is a dark rectangular patch above the doorknob, and beneath it there is part of a circle. Along the edge of the door two bolts show.

f) The leg of the seat is unfinished at the lower end.

Part XVI · Plate 32 · Page 508

Mr. Dombey and the World

[PLATE A]

a) The signatures of the two plates are very similar. The *P* of the name is separated from the *H*, and the *Z* ends in a line extending under the name to the left.

b) The masthead of the paper shows letters something like "Tmna."

c) Mr. Pitt "on the bust," as Mark Twain would have it, has a topknot.

d) Major Bagstock's coat shows four buttons.

e) The fingers of Cousin Feenix's left hand do not quite touch his chin.

[PLATE B]

a) The signature appears as though it were spelled "RII3." There is no cross-bar to the *H*, and there is a small circle at the end of the last stroke of the *Z*.

b) The masthead is not readable.

c) Mr. Pitt is bald.

d) Major Bagstock's coat has three buttons.

e) The fingers of Cousin Feenix's left hand touch his chin.

Mr. Dombey and the World

Mr. Dombey and the World

Part XVII · Plate 33 · Page 516

Secret Intelligence

[P L A T E A]

a) The signatures in the two plates are very similar. In Plate A it ends in a very small hook at the left.
b) The shading of the pitcher hanging from the shelf at the right is in lines parallel to its axis.
c) The cloth hanging to the right of this pitcher is shaded mostly with vertical lines.
d) The table leg shows partly white.
e) The upper part of the left inner line of the door frame is single.

[P L A T E B]

a) Below the lower line of the Z in the signature there is a mark that looks like a P and a period.
b) The pitcher is shaded, partly parallel to its axis and partly with vertical lines.
c) The cloth at the right is shaded with diagonal lines.
d) The table leg is dark.
e) The line of the left door frame on the side of the opening is double.

Secret intelligence?

Part XVII · Plate 34 · Page 539

Mr. Carker in His Hour of Triumph

[P L A T E   A]

a) The signature is plain, with the final line of the *Z* ending in a straight line to the left.

b) In the legend the letter *t* of *triumph* begins with an upstroke.

c) The left corbel of the mantel is shaded and clearly defined.

d) The candle at the extreme right does not show hot wax running down the side.

e) The Amazon's horse at the right is shaded by horizontal lines.

f) The toppiece of the chair behind Edith is shaded in only the upper portion by vertical lines.

[P L A T E   B]

a) The signature is clean cut and ends with a loop, open downward.

b) In the legend the letter *t* begins with a downstroke.

c) The left corbel of the mantel is only faintly sketched.

d) The candle shows a drop of wax at the side.

e) The Amazon's horse is shaded by vertical lines.

f) The chair behind Edith has the top crosspiece shaded by horizontal lines.

Mr Carker in his hour of triumph

Mr Carker in his hour of triumph

On the Dark Road

This is the fourth horizontal plate in *Dombey* and the first of the so-called "dark plates" which were produced by first machine-engraving the entire plate with a series of fine parallel lines, then coating it with wax, and etching the design through this wax. The plates are thus a combination of steel engraving and etching. The process was apparently satisfactory, but for some reason or other it was not used again until Plate 31 of *David Copperfield* appeared. Thereafter, in *Bleak House* there were ten and in *Little Dorritt*, eight.

[P L A T E   A]

a) There are dots before and above the signature. The flourish following the letter *Z* ends at the left in a sharp angle and a short upturn. The upper line of the *Z* is straight.

b) The whiplash ends above the white streak near the horizon.

c) The strap extending from the mouth of the off horse to the white one is shown more than halfway by a double line. The rein shown between the neck and the tail is single.

[P L A T E   B]

a) The flourish at the end of the *Z* extends below the *P* of *Phiz* and turns upward in a sharp angle, to end in a loop and a tail that touches the letter *P*.

b) The whiplash ends just as it touches the white line of the clouds.

c) The strap between the two leading horses is shown by only a single line, while the rein between neck and tail of the off horse is double.

In the dark Road

On the dark Road.

An Arrival

Only a contortionist could twist his body as Mr. Toots does, but, except for the caricature of Sol Gills, the plate is excellent.

[PLATE A]

a) The letter *Z* begins and ends in flourishes, extending to the left into a wiggly tail.

b) The drawings on the screen clearly show figures, that in the center of two persons, that at the right of something with wings.

c) Gill's stock shows no pattern.

d) The girl at the left has only a small button at the ends of her collar, and her embroidery frame shows numerous parallel lines on the back.

e) The yarn from the ball below the dog's left foot passes under the spool, swings to the scissors, and then divides into two parts, the upper one making similar curves but ending at the left of the two buttons, halfway between these and the sewing box.

[PLATE B]

a) The signatures in the two plates are similar. Plate B shows the letter *Z*, beginning with a straight horizontal line, making it look like a figure 3. The tail swings under the word *PHIZ* and ends at the left in a flourish. There are also two very small wavy lines in the lower left, outside the floor shading, that resemble figures 2.

b) The drawings on the screen are too sketchy to identify.

c) Sol Gills's stock shows several small circles.

d) The girl at the extreme left wears a brooch, and the embroidery frame in her hands shows three vertical and two horizontal lines on the back.

e) The cord from the ball of yarn below the dog's left foot passes above the spool, than crosses the scissors, makes a loop, swings back in a wiggly line, and ends at one of the buttons.

An arrival.

An arrival

"Let Him Remember It in That Room, Years to Come!"

[PLATE A]

a) The *Z* in the signature begins with a horizontal line and ends in a loop, open to the left.
b) Mr. Pitt's topknot is somewhat upstanding.
c) The upper part of the door is shaded simply with vertical lines.
d) The left hand of Miss Tox shows her thumb.
e) The top of the lamp held by the cupid who had never been to West Point ends in a serrated edge.
f) The lower figure in the middle panel of the screen is too sketchy to be determined.
g) On the table the envelope with a seal lying near the front rests upon another envelope.
h) The *h* of *him* in the legend begins with a downstroke.

[PLATE B]

a) The *Z* of the signature begins with a circle open at the bottom and ends with a wiggly line to the right. In front of the *P* the line extends to the left and is there crossed by a disconnected curve, so that the whole signature looks like "*F.PHIZ*."
b) Mr. Pitt's topknot has been flattened out.
c) The upper part of the door is shaded by both horizontal and vertical lines.
d) The left hand of Miss Tox shows no thumb.
e) The top of the lamp is cut off smoothly.
f) The lower figure in the middle panel of the screen seems to be a fat hog going into the picture.
g) The envelope on the table has no other below it.
h) The *h* of *him* in the legend begins with an upstroke.

"Let him remember it in that room, years to come!"

"Let him remember it in that room, years to come!"

Another Wedding

This is the fifth horizontal plate, an orientation which gave "Phiz" a free hand in etching this amusing and superb illustration.

[P L A T E A]

a) The *Z* of the signature begins with a horizontal line and ends in a line to the left and a curve resembling a 3.
b) The theater poster at the lower left shows a number *1* in its lower corner. It may or may not be the plate number.
c) The poster above this one shows tolls for cow and pig at the bottom of the list.
d) Captain Cuttle has two shirt buttons showing.
e) The first poster to the right of the cigar-store Indian gives the name of the schooner as *Wasp*. The *z* in *Amazon* is reversed in the next poster.
f) The shade lines on the trousers of the boy at the extreme right are diagonal.
g) The tails of the two chickens at the right of the lower center do not quite touch.

[P L A T E B]

a) The *z* of the signature begins with a curve open to the left and ends with a curve, a little loop, a line below the entire signature, and an upturned double curve.
b) The theater poster at the lower left shows no number in the corner.
c) The poster above this gives tolls for only three kinds of animals.
d) Only one button or breast pin shows on Captain Cuttle's shirt.
e) The schooner's name on the poster back of the Indian is *Triumph*. Below this is the name *Carl Bing*.
f) The shade lines on the boy's trousers are horizontal.
g) The tails of the two chickens touch.

Another wedding.

Another wedding

Part XX · Plate 39 · Frontispiece

This plate, giving a summary of the events in the story, goes in rather heavily for Paul among the angels, of whom only three have feathered wings.

[PLATE A]

a) The signature is left of the lower center. There are three dots, one preceding the signature, one after it, and one above the space between the *H* and the *I*.

b) Most of the body of the fat mermaid or merman at the bottom of the picture is shaded.

c) There is only one button on the back of the peajacket of the man on his hands and knees, below Florence's hat.

d) There are only two lines radiating from the locket on Florence's breast.

e) The little sketch of Dombey near the cashbox and above and to the left of the guardian angels does not show his feet.

f) There are only two rays above the head of the angel with its arm raised, but apparently there is another touching its arm.

g) The angel at the left, above the deathbed of Paul, has no rays above her head. Most of the Celestial Choir seem to be females, although the Bible mentions only male angels.

h) The woman back of Mr. Dombey at the right center shows two hands.

[PLATE B]

a) The signature has a figure *2* and a dot before it.

b) The fat merman's body is shaded only at the right.

c) The man on his hands and knees has two buttons on the back of his jacket.

d) There are two lines, besides the two of the chain, radiating from Florence's locket.

e) Dombey's left foot shows.

f) There are four rays above the angel's head.

g) The angel at the left has three rays above her head.

h) The woman back of Mr. Dombey, at the right, shows only one hand.

Part XX · Plate 40 · Title-page

As has often been mentioned, the hook, by mistake, is on Captain Cuttle's left arm. Below this vignette is the publishers' imprint: London/Bradbury & Evans, Bouverie Street./1848.

[PLATE A]

a) The signature below the vignette shows a small *1* as a subscript to the *H*. It may possibly be intended for a plate number.
b) The blunderbuss is shaded by horizontal lines.
c) The glasses on the shelf above the candle are well defined.
d) There are two buttons in the upholstery on the back of Captain Cuttle's chair.

[PLATE B]

a) The signature has a curlicue, which looks like the figure 3, attached to the left downstroke of the *H*. There is a dot within a circle above the *I* and also a dot after the *H*. Above the wavy line preceding the *P* there is an abortive *2*.
b) The blunderbuss is shaded by diagonal lines.
c) The glasses on the shelf above the candle are sketchy.
d) No buttons show on the back of Captain Cuttle's chair, although there is a small black dot a bit higher up.

DEALINGS WITH THE FIRM

OF

DOMBEY AND SON,

Wholesale, Retail and for Exportation.

BY

Charles Dickens.

LONDON
BRADBURY & EVANS, BOUVERIE STREET
1848

DEALINGS WITH THE FIRM

OF

DOMBEY AND SON,

Wholesale, Retail and for Exportation.

BY

Charles Dickens.

LONDON
BRADBURY & EVANS, BOUVERIE STREET
1848.

The
Personal History
of
DAVID COPPERFIELD

Dombey and Son ended in April, 1848, and in May, 1849, *David Copperfield* was begun. It followed the mode of issue of the preceding novels and appeared in monthly parts, the last two, Nos. 19 and 20, being published in November, 1850. There were 40 etchings, all in duplicate. Hatton and Cleaver say that no plate was numbered, but actually a few were, as, for example, the second Plate 2. None of the plates was lithographed.

For some reason or other, the etching of many of the plates for this book was not as successful as for the preceding novels, and they lack atmosphere, so that the printing of the backgrounds are as heavy as the foregrounds. The prints thus have more the appearance of "zinc etchings" than of plates pulled from steels. Perhaps Browne left the etching more and more to his assistants, as he certainly did the printing. This letdown in the plates is more noticeable in the succeeding novels and especially in *A Tale of Two Cities*.

In *David Copperfield* there were 21 horizontal plates, one of them being the second "dark plate" made by Browne for Dickens' novels. No further dark plates were issued for *David Copperfield*, but 10 appeared in *Bleak House* and 8 in *Little Dorrit*. The plate paper used for the etchings of *David Copperfield* appears to be of better quality than usual and still remains perfectly white in most cases, and foxing is at a minimum.

While Dickens was resting after the completion of *Dombey and Son*, in April, 1948, and before *David Copperfield* began to appear in May, 1849, "Phiz" etched 12 plates for W. Blanchard Jerrold's *Disgrace to the Family*, made 28 drawings for Reach's *Romance of a Mince Pie*, and etched at least 10 plates for miscellaneous works. While *David Copperfield* was being issued, he etched 80 plates for that work, 29 for Lever's *Con Cregan*, 40 for Lever's *Roland Cashel*, frontispieces for four of Bulwer's novels, and 21 woodcuts for James's *Fight of the Fiddlers*, besides some plates and cuts for less important works.

Part I · Plate 1 · Page 11

Our Pew at Church

The signatures of the artist are alike in the two plates, both being in capital letters and shown at the bottom of the "resurgam" tombstone. The second plate is numbered twice in Arabic numerals in the lower right corner. Plate 1 is one of the best of the etchings in *David Copperfield*.

[PLATE A]

a) The man in the niche at the upper right has his pen in his left hand. He is looking straight ahead.

b) The space below the architrave and above the Bodgers' inscription and between the two cherubs is blank.

c) In the diamond-shaped shield at the top center, the ribbon at the bottom is actually a snake or an eel.

d) Just below the choir the list of benefactors of the church is headed by . . . *Smooce Esq. 1000.*

e) In the upper left corner, the cherub with the spider hanging from its horn does not touch the horn to his mouth. The sign below reads *GLORY FAMA.*

f) The chinless priest has a ring on the little finger of his right hand.

g) The man outside the gate in the lower left has two stripes on the back of his glove.

[PLATE B]

a) The man in the niche at the upper right has his pen in his right hand.

b) The space below the architrave is shaded by horizontal lines.

c) The diamond-shaped shield has the ornamentation so arranged that it shows a smiling face. On the ribbon the letters *VIRT* and *TI* can be distinguished.

d) The list of benefactors is headed by *Sir . . Dunousle 300* (the name is not perfectly clear).

e) The horn comes from the mouth of the cherub with the spider.

f) The priest has no ring.

g) There are three lines of stitching on the back of the right glove of the man in the lower left corner.

Our Pew at Church

Part I · Plate 2 · Page 23

I Am Hospitably Received by Mr. Peggotty

This horizontal plate was etched in duplicate. As in the title-page, here also the boat is incorrectly turned upside down, quite possibly originally to make a better picture, and throughout the book it remained uncorrected by Dickens. There are many differences in shading between the two plates.

[P L A T E   A]

a) The signature is small, with one dot over and one dot after it. The Z begins with a straight line and ends with a single loop at the left.
b) The back of the chair upon which Miss Peggotty is leaning shows no central ornament in the top rail, but at the left there is a distinct letter N. The central vertical part of the chair shows a small oval cutout.
c) The arched ribs of the boat, as well as the crossbeam above Mr. Peggotty's head, show no zigzag lines of shading.
d) The plate is not numbered.

[P L A T E   B]

a) The signature shows more ornamentation than that in Plate A.
b) The back of Miss Peggotty's chair shows a circle in the top crosspiece but no oval in the vertical part.
c) The ribs and the beam of the boat show zigzag and vertical lines of shading.
d) There is a small 2 after the signature and a curve that may be a 2 above it. There is also an angular 2 or a Z below the toy tank (?) on the floor.

I am hospitably received by Mr. Peggotty.

I am hospitably received by Mr. Peggotty.

The Friendly Waiter and I

[PLATE A]

a) The *H* of the artist's signature has a crossbar; the *Z* begins with a straight, horizontal line at the top and ends below with a small loop and a straight line extending to the left.

b) The top of the frame of the *Sancho Panza* picture has a single line above two horizontal lines. The name is given below the picture.

c) The fox and the crane picture shows no ornament in the lower left corner of the frame, and the frame itself shows little carving at the four corners.

d) Below the *Directory* on the mantel there are four short vertical lines marking the end of the fireplace above the steam.

e) The opening of the fireplace is shown by a single line at the top, and above this there are three horizontal lines dying out into two at the right.

f) At the upper left, the map of Yorkshire has several vertical lines; the map itself shows no face.

g) In the Mercator map of the world, the British Islés are shown simply as some scratchy lines.

[PLATE B]

a) The *H* in the signature is not crossed. The upper line of the *Z* begins at the left with a small hook, and the letter ends in a line to the left with a terminal hook like a figure 2.

b) Sancho Panza's picture is not labeled, and the frame shows a pair of double lines along the top.

c) The fox and crane picture shows an **S**-shaped ornament in the lower left corner, and the four corners show carving.

d) The steam from the dinner conceals the corner of the mantel.

e) A double line forms the top of the fireplace opening, and above that there are two sharply defined horizontal lines.

f) The upper part of the left side of the Yorkshire map is shown by a single line, and the map itself shows a face at the left.

g) In the Mercator map the position of the British Isles is shown by the face of a man with his thumb to his nose and his fingers extended.

The friendly Waiter and I.

The friendly Waiter and I.

Part II · Plate 4 · Page 55

My Musical Breakfast

[PLATE A]

a) There is a small curve at the beginning of the *Z* in *PHIZ* and a loop at the left end.
b) The bowl below the cracked mirror shows vestiges of lettering.
c) There are five boards in the wall cutting off the stairway, each board separated from its neighbor by a single line.
d) The horizontal pieces of the back of the "old woman's" chair (not Mrs. Fibbitson's) are shaded by vertical lines.
e) The flowerpot back of the "Master" is shaded by diagonal lines except for a small portion at the left.

[PLATE B]

a) The name *PHIZ* begins with a vertical line in front of the *P*. The last letter begins with a loop and, after it swings beneath the signature, ends in a loop and a tie.
b) The bowl below the mirror shows a curved line as ornamentation.
c) The stairway boards are separated by lines which are double most of the way.
d) The crosspieces of the old woman's chair are shaded by horizontal lines.
e) The flowerpot is shaded by horizontal lines.

My musical breakfast.

My musical breakfast.

a) The *P* of the signature is preceded by a curve. The *Z* is rather complicated but ends at the left below the signature, where it intersects the middle of a short, straight line.

b) There are just a few scratches above the books. Below, there are a few letters followed by *Jim Stylz is a donkey*.

c) The box is marked *Snob, I am* [?] *his box. No it an't*. The box at the right is marked *Snooks* and *Sam*.

d) The desk is marked *Has your mother sold . . . mangle*.

e) The eyes of *See-Sir* look straight ahead.

f) The man in the doorway wears no nightcap. The man with the wooden leg has five buttons on his vest, and the stripes are made by double lines.

g) There are nine marbles.

h) Steerforth has only one shirt button.

i) The bench is marked *Si, DT, Tom Inms*, and *Brown*. Nothing below the hole (or is this really an apple?) in the bench.

Part III · Plate 5 · Page 70

Steerforth and Mr. Mell

Of such small differences as those given below do the points of separation consist. There were two steels, neither with numbers.

[P L A T E   A]

a) The *P* of the signature is preceded by a vertical line. The *Z* begins at the top with a horizontal straight line and ends below the *P* in a hook.

b) Above the books on the high shelf, there are rather rudimentary letters forming the name *David I*. Beneath the shelf are the words *Jim Styles*.

c) The box at the left is marked *Snob, His Box. No, it an't*. The box to the right of this one is marked *Snooks. Sammy*.

d) The desk is marked *Has your mother sol . . . il* [?] *mangle*.

e) The eyes of *See-Sir, A Rumun*, are turned toward his left side.

f) In the doorway the man at the left wears a nightcap. The man with a wooden leg at the right has only three buttons on his vest, which is shown with single-line stripes.

g) Including the one near David's foot, there are seven marbles on the floor.

h) Steerforth has two buttons in his shirt front.

i) The tilted bench is marked *A* [*or R*] *Young; J. Taylor; H.C.B.: J. Smith; W.G.R.B. 4th* and several other initials.

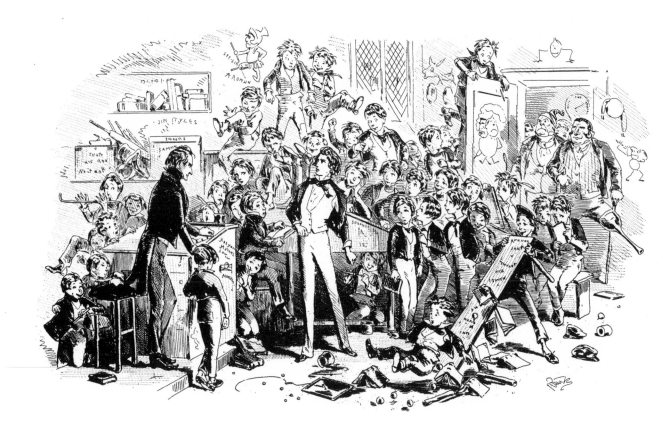

Steerforth and Mr. Mell

Steerforth and Mr. Mell.

Changes at Home

This plate was etched in duplicate, neither numbered. As a drawing, "Phiz" failed to make it interesting. Artistically it lacks balance and has no center of interest.

[P L A T E   A]

a) The second stroke of the letter *Z* forms the crossline of the *H* also. The signature ends in a line to the left.
b) The rectangular plates above and below the doorknob are defined at the top and bottom by short horizontal lines.
c) There is a $\frac{3}{8}$-inch vertical line in the right margin, below the lower edge of the door.
d) David's left sock is white.
e) The lady in the oval frame has locks which come down over her ears, making it impossible to see whether she wears earrings.
f) The top of the book on the table behind David's mother is shaded by parallel lines.
g) There are two figures behind the prodigal son in the picture at the left.

[P L A T E   B]

a) The last line of the *Z* in the signature ends in a loop at the left. The crossline of the *H* is parallel to the first line of the *Z* and extends through the *P* as well.
b) There are no top and bottom lines to the lower doorplate.
c) There is no vertical line in the margin near the bottom of the door.
d) Both David's socks are shaded by diagonal lines.
e) The lady in the oval frame has earrings.
f) The top of the book behind David's mother is white.
g) There is only one figure between the fatted calf and the prodigal son.

Changes at Home.

Changes at Home.

Part IV · Plate 7 · Page 105

Mrs. Gummidge Casts a Damp on Our Departure

This illustration is unusually successful for a *Copperfield* plate. As usual, however, Peggotty's boathouse is shown bottom up and not as described in the text.

[P L A T E   A]

a) The upper line of the *Z* in *PHIZ* is straight, the tail is a line swinging to the left with a small loop below the *I*, then extending $\frac{1}{4}$ inch beyond the *P* and ending in an open loop, above which is a short, wavy line.
b) The script engraver has crossed the *t* in *casts* in the legend in the usual way, but in *departure* he has used the German style.
c) There are two birds in the sky at the upper left and one over the sea. The sky line shows six sails.
d) At the right end of the "house" the oval window is entirely covered by the fishnet.

[P L A T E   B]

a) The *Z* of the signature begins with a curve resembling a figure 2 and ends with a small loop, within which it again closes in a circle.
b) Both *t*'s are crossed in the legend.
c) There is one bird in the sky to the left and one over the sea. The sky line shows three sails and a couple of dots above the horizon.
d) The oval window is now in the upper middle of the end of the boat and is only half-covered by the fishnet.

Mrs Gummidge casts a damp on our departure.

Mrs. Gummidge casts a damp on our departure

My magnificent order at the public-house

Part IV · Plate 8 · Page 116

My Magnificent Order at the Public-House

In spite of being cluttered with details, the plate is good.

[P L A T E   A]

a) The signature looks like "RII3," the tail of the Z having a little loop before continuing straight to the left. There is a sickle-like curve after the name.

b) The *t* in the word *the* of the legend is not crossed, the *h* beginning at its side.

c) The beer mug lying in the pile on the floor, whose lip is directly below the middle of the *Soda Water* lettering, shows its open top.

d) The wine poster at the left shows at the top an indeterminable line of lettering, below which is the word *WINES*, whose top and bottom are limited by horizontal lines. Below this is a line beginning *IN* but ending in indistinguishable letters.

e) There is no pedestal under Bacchus in the window.

f) The left funnel on the mantel has a straight stem.

[P L A T E   B]

a) The signature is very similar to that in Plate A, except that the final line of the *Z*, after it starts to swing to the left, forms a small loop on its upper side and continues to the left, where, with an acute angle, it returns downward in three-quarters of a circle and, as it swings upward, crosses the tail of the *Z*.

b) The *t*'s in the legend are all crossed.

c) The beer mug in the middle shows the bottom and not the open top.

d) The wine poster reads *J. Philpot. Wines in bottles*.

e) There is a square pedestal under Bacchus which extends down behind the bottles.

f) The left funnel has a tube curved on the side toward the mug.

My magnificent order at the public-house.

Part V · Plate 9 · Page 137

I Make Myself Known to My Aunt

This plate, like No. 6, is not a successful composition artistically, although one writer considered it the best in the book!

[PLATE A]

a) Two of the initial *m*'s in the legend begin below the line, while that of *myself* starts higher up.

b) The curved chair back (?), which is seen through the window, is shaded by horizontal lines.

c) The boy on the donkey in the background at the left is shaded across his shoulders; the underside of the bucking donkey is somewhat shaded; and the stick in the hand of the boy back of the donkey is shown by parallel lines.

d) The eye of Aunt Betsy is wide open and staring.

[PLATE B]

a) All the *m*'s begin below the line.

b) The curved object in the window is shaded by vertical lines.

c) The boy in the distance, as well as the mule at his right, is unshaded. The stick in the hand of the other boy is shown as a single line.

d) Aunt Betsy's eye is not so staring.

I make myself known to my Aunt.

I make myself known to my Aunt.

Part V · Plate 10 · Page 149

The Momentous Interview

[P L A T E A]

a) In the legend the crossline of the letter *t* in *interview* extends to the left of the main stem.

b) The picture on the wall shows the words *Joseps Garmen*. Five of Joseph's brethren are shown.

c) The smoke from the boat seen through the window extends to the right.

d) Miss Murdstone's chair is lightly shaded in the back, and the back leg seen under the chair is faintly sketched.

e) Miss Murdstone's veil shown an ornament at the lower end that looks like a pollywog below a bent arrow.

f) Mr. Murdstone's chair back, below his elbow, is shaded only by light diagonal lines.

[P L A T E B]

a) The crossline of the letter *t* in *interview* stops at the main stem.

b) The picture on the wall shows the words *Joseph Garment*. There are only four of his brethren shown.

c) The smoke from the distant boat extends to the left.

d) Miss Murdstone's chair back is heavily shaded, and the back leg seen under the chair is shaded by vertical lines.

e) Miss Murdstone's veil shows an ornament which is a distinct figure *2*, seemingly too plain to be simply accidental.

f) Mr. Murdstone's chair back below his elbow is shaded by vertical as well as by diagonal lines.

The momentous interview

The momentous interview

I Return to the Doctor's after the Party

[P L A T E   A]

a) The two signatures are very much alike except that Plate A has the end of the *Z* finished off by a hook downward.
b) There is a doorknob on the door.
c) There are no shade lines across the top of the "Brick Babylon."
d) The mantel at the right shows some ornamental work.

[P L A T E   B]

a) The *Z* of the signature is finished with an upcurve at the end of the lower line.
b) There is no doorknob.
c) There are vertical shade lines across the brick.
d) The mantel is very sketchily drawn.

I return to the Doctor's after the party

I return to the Doctor's after the party

Somebody turns the

Part VI · Plate 12 · Page 182

Somebody Turns Up

[P L A T E   A]

a) The lower line of the *Z* in the signature swings to the left with a loop, and then, beyond, the name ends in a complicated wiggle.

b) There is a ghostly cat showing below Uriah Heep's chair, apparently an early sketch intended later to be burnished out, for the floor lines show through it.

c) The teakettle in the fireplace is shaded by diagonal lines.

d) The judge's picture at the right shows a robe shaded by diagonal lines.

[P L A T E   B]

a) The signature ends in a fairly straight line, without a loop, at the left. There are three dots before the *P*.

b) There is no cat's ghost shown under Uriah Heep's chair.

c) The teakettle is shaded by vertical lines.

d) The picture on the wall at the right shows no shading on the judge's robe.

Somebody turns up.

Part VII · Plate 13 · Page 201

My First Fall in Life

This is a good, well-balanced drawing, although, if the distant road and trees were more lightly etched, the effect would be better.

[PLATE A]

a) The signature ends in a loopless, slightly curved line at the left.
b) There is one bird in the sky at the right but none at the top center.
c) David's scarf does not show a loose end. His coat shows three buttons on his left side and only some dots on his right.
d) There is a man on horseback in the road far away.
e) There is nothing between the head of the horse at the left and the fence.

[PLATE B]

a) The signature shows a wavy line beneath it.
b) There are three birds in the upper central portion of the sky.
c) David's scarf shows a loose end. His coat has two buttons on each side.
d) In the road in the distance there is a woman in a cape and possibly a man beyond, under a tree.
e) Between the head of the horse at the left and the bottom of the fence there is a symbol which may represent a *W* right side up or a figure *2* lying on its side.

My first fall in life.

My first fall in life.

We Arrive Unexpectedly at Mr. Peggotty's Fireside

As usual, the boat is incorrectly drawn upside down.

[P L A T E   A]

a) The shading of the picture above Ham's head is diagonal.

b) The tray or mirror above the dresser shows a picture of some sort.

c) The mug on the table between Mr. Peggotty and Mrs. Gummidge is shaded by vertical lines.

d) No plate shows back of Mrs. Gummidge's head.

e) The diagonal shade lines on Steerforth's and David's faces slant downward from left to right.

f) There are three distinct nails and two lines representing part of a handle in the end of the chest at the lower right.

g) The back of Emily's bonnet on the chest is shaded by diagonal lines.

[P L A T E   B]

a) The shading of the picture above Ham's head is by vertical and horizontal lines.

b) There is no design on the mirror.

c) The mug on the table is shaded by diagonal lines.

d) There is a curve back of Mrs. Gummidge's head, indicating a plate.

e) The shade lines on Steerforth's and David's faces slant downward slightly from right to left.

f) There are traces of at least four nails in the end of the chest. The handle is indicated only by a single short line.

g) The back of Emily's bonnet is shaded by curved lines slanting downward from right to left.

We arrive unexpectedly at M.͟ Peggotty's fireside.

We arrive unexpectedly at Mr. Peggotty's fireside.

Part VIII · Plate 15 · Page 233

I Make the Acquaintance of Miss Mowcher

[P L A T E   A]

a) The signature ends in a line with one jog to the left.
b) The upper right part of the picture of the wreck is shaded only by diagonal lines.
c) In the next picture Dr. Faust wears baggy pantaloons. Gretchen has her left hand near her chin. The cords holding the picture are broken and not continuous to the ceiling, and there is no hook for the cord.
d) One of the seven Sutherland sisters is hung by one cord.
e) There are four Brobdingnagians with Gulliver.

[P L A T E   B]

a) The signature ends in a long flourish to the left.
b) The wreck is shaded at the upper right by both diagonal and horizontal lines.
c) Dr. Faust wears no baggy trousers, only trunks. Gretchen has her left hand at her waist. The cords holding the picture frame are continuous and extend to a hook at the cornice.
d) The long-haired lady is hung by two cords.
e) There are only three Brobdingnagians with Gulliver.

I make the acquaintance of Miss Mowcher.

I make the acquaintance of Miss Mowcher.

Part VIII · Plate 16 · Page 238

Martha

[P L A T E   A]

a) The signature ends in a closed loop at the left.
b) In the picture above the mantel, Jesus is shaded by horizontal, as well as by short vertical, lines, and the space below his feet and above the lines of the frame is shaded horizontally.
c) In the picture of Eve and the serpent, the head of the latter is clearly shown.
d) The clock shows the hour hand at five o'clock.
e) There is a candle end in the flat candlestick on the mantel.

[P L A T E   B]

a) The signature ends in a long scrawl to the left.
b) The shading of Jesus' robe is vertical, and the space below his feet is blank.
c) The serpent's head is obscured by foliage.
d) The clock shows no hand at five o'clock.
e) There is no candle in the flat candlestick.

Martha.

Martha.

338 / COPPERFIELD *Plates 16A and 16B*

Part IX · Plate 17 · Page 262

Uriah Persists in Hovering near Us at the Dinner Party

In the List of Illustrations the page number for this plate is given as 262, and it is inserted at that place in the book. Actually, the event shown occurs on page 265.

[P L A T E   A]

a) The signature has a short, sharp hook at the end of a straight line to the left.
b) In the legend the *i* of *in* and the *n* of *near* begin at the base line.
c) "Buttons," between David and Uriah, has only one row of buttons on his coat.
d) The women sitting back of Traddles are shaded by vertical lines.

[P L A T E   B]

a) The signature shows an upcurve like the figure 2 at the left end of the tail line.
b) In the legend the letters *i* and *n* in *in* and *near* begin below the base line.
c) The boy between David and Uriah has three rows of buttons on his coat.
d) The first two women back of Traddles are shaded by horizontal lines, the third by diagonals.

Uriah persists in hovering near us, at the dinner party.

Uriah persists in hovering near us, at the dinner party.

Part IX · Plate 18 · Page 274

I Fall into Captivity

This etching is less successful than usual. The women's dresses and the background are extremely scratchy. Dora is well drawn and shows her coquettish character in her eyes. In the text David spoke of her as "rather diminutive"; therefore, he himself must have been decidedly taller, although he is not so shown in this illustration. In Plate 28 he is a head taller.

[P L A T E   A]

a) The c in the word *captivity* in the legend begins at the top.
b) The music book on the piano shows no vertical lines on the left page.
c) There is no flower on the floor below Dora.

[P L A T E   B]

a) The c of *captivity* begins with an upstroke.
b) The music book shows three short vertical lines on the left-hand page.
c) There is a flower at Dora's feet.

I fall into captivity!

I fall into captivity.

Part X · Plate 19 · Page 292

We Are Disturbed in Our Cookery

[PLATE A]

a) The *Z* of the signature ends in a line to the left with a single loop.
b) In the picture on the wall, Damocles' topknot stands upright. The wine jug and goblet are not well shown.
c) The cup on the mantel has no handle.
d) There is a curved line of smoke, which looks like the figure 3, beneath the gridiron in Mr. Micawber's hand.
e) The plate in Traddles' hand is shaded by vertical lines.

[PLATE B]

a) The last line of the *Z* in the signature has no loop.
b) Damocles' topknot bends downward. The jug and goblet are clearly shown.
c) The cup on the mantel has a handle.
d) There is no smoke beneath the gridiron, but the curved line resembling the figure 3 has risen and is now above it and to the right.
e) The plate in Traddles' hand is shaded by horizontal lines.

Plate 18B   COPPERFIELD / 343

We are disturbed in our cookery.

We are disturbed in our cookery.

Part X · Plate 20 · Page 313

I Find Mr. Barkis "Going Out with the Tide"

[P L A T E   A]

a) The signature ends in a wavy line without a loop but with a small, turned-down hook at the end.

b) In the legend the *a* of *Barkis* begins with an upstroke.

c) The cord of the hanging bookshelves extends to a knot at the nail and then back downward to the left for a short distance. The book at the left, as well as the one lying flat, is shaded by horizontal lines.

d) The bed canopy is shaded at the top by vertical and diagonal lines, as well as by vertical and horizontal dots.

e) The top of the mirror is shaded by vertical and diagonal lines.

f) The meeting rail of the window is shown by three parallel lines.

[P L A T E   B]

a) The signature ends in a long scrawl to the left.

b) The *a* of *Barkis* in the legend begins with a downstroke.

c) Only a single line is shown for the cord holding the bookcase. No book is shaded by horizontal lines.

d) The bed canopy is shaded by vertical lines and horizontal dots.

e) The top of the mirror has a few horizontal lines, but the greater part of the shading is by vertical lines.

f) The meeting rail of the window sash is shown by two parallel lines.

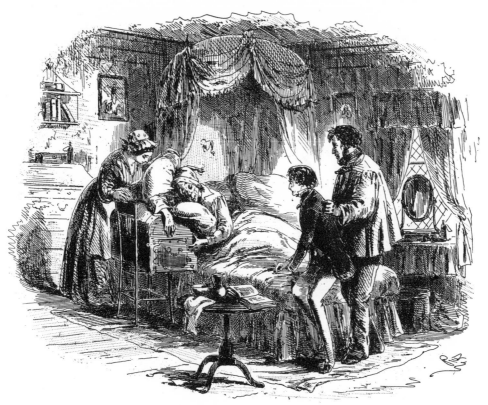

I find M^r. Barkis "going out with the tide."

I find Mr. Barkis "going out with the tide."

Mr Peggotty and Mr Steerforth.

Part XI · Plate 21 · Page 330

Mr. Peggotty and Mrs. Steerforth

[P L A T E   A]

a) The signature ends at the left in a very small, sharp hook.
b) The vertical shade lines leave most of Apollo's face unshaded.
c) There are no shade lines across the face of the clock.
d) The right arm of the child in the large picture above the mantel is not shaded.

[P L A T E   B]

a) The flourish at the end of the signature makes a complete loop around it.
b) Apollo's face is shaded by vertical lines.
c) There are two vertical lines across the face of the clock.
d) The right arm of the child in the picture is shaded.

Mr. Peggotty and Mrs. Steerforth.

Part XI · Plate 22 · Page 350

My Aunt Astonishes Me

[PLATE A]

a) The *Z* in the signature cuts across the *H* and *I* and ends below in a line to the left.
b) The trunk upon which Aunt Betsy has her feet shows many nailheads.
c) The top of the chair at the extreme left has multiple lines, and the left line of the upright part is a double line.
d) The cord by which the picture at the left is hung does not reach the frame. The background of the girl in the picture is not shaded on the left side.
e) There are diagonal shade lines on David's nose.

[PLATE B]

a) The *Z* in the signature ends in three-fourths of a circle, with a small loop at the left, but the extreme end does not extend to the left as far as the letter itself.
b) The trunk upon which Aunt Betsy's feet rest shows no nailheads.
c) The chair at the left is outlined on the side and top by single lines.
d) The picture cord reaches the frame on both sides and is fashioned into a loop at the upper end.
e) David's nose is white.

My Aunt astonishes me.

My Aunt astonishes me

Mr. Wickfield and His Partner Wait upon My Aunt

[P L A T E   A]

a) The signature takes a new form, the first line of the *H* being connected at the bottom with the stem of the *P*. The *Z* ends in an irregular wavy line a short distance to the left of the *P*.
b) The picture frame of the castle is shaded at the top and partly at the sides by vertical lines.
c) The second picture is a well-defined bust portrait of a girl.
d) There is no stick supporting the right-hand plant in the window.
e) Mr. Wickfield's vest shows only three buttons.
f) The lower line of Aunt Betsy's apron does not cross the cloth in her lap.
g) The plate is not numbered.

[P L A T E   B]

a) The lower line of the *Z* in the signature goes to the left, makes a complete loop, and then is extended $\frac{3}{4}$ inch as a wiggly line to the left.
b) The picture frame is shaded at the top and partly at the sides by diagonal as well as vertical lines.
c) The second picture is more or less lost in the shading.
d) The second plant in the window is supported by a stick.
e) Mr. Wickfield's vest shows four buttons.
f) The lower line of Aunt Betsy's apron was drawn, by mistake, across the cloth in her lap.
g) There is a faint figure *2* in the left margin opposite Uriah Heep's right foot. The number is too plain to be an accidental scratch on the plate.

Mʳ Wickfield and his partner wait upon my Aunt.

Mr Wickfield and his partner wait upon my Aunt

Part XII · Plate 24 · Page 378

Mr. Micawber Delivers Some Valedictory Remarks

[P L A T E   A]

a) The signature ends with a short curve and a final closed circle under the *H* of *PHIZ*. The *H* has no crossbar.

b) There is no spoon in the bowl on the shelf above the children's heads.

c) Both glasses back of Mrs. Micawber's left hand carry spoons.

d) There is a button in David's shirt front.

e) There is a hat below Traddles' chair.

f) There is no flame on the candle between David and Micawber.

g) The flame on the candle back of Micawber inclines upward and to the left.

h) The bowl adjacent to the bottle back of Micawber has a spoon in it.

i) There is a circle in the upper crosspiece of Mrs. Micawber's chair.

j) There is a tray of dishes and oyster shells back of Traddles' chair.

[P L A T E   B]

a) The *Z* of the signature ends in a curve which turns upward at the left end and touches the *P*.

b) There is a spoon in the bowl on the shelf over the children's heads.

c) The glass nearest Mrs. Micawber's right hand has no spoon.

d) There is no button on David's shirt.

e) There is no hat below Traddles' chair.

f) The candle in front of Micawber has a flame.

g) The candle back of Micawber has its flame straight up.

h) The bowl above Traddles' head has no spoon in it.

i) There is no circle in the back of Mrs. Micawber's chair.

j) There is no tray back of Traddles' chair, but in its place there is an oblong parcel.

Mr. Micawber delivers some valedictory remarks.

Mr. Micawber delivers some valedictory remarks.

Part XIII · Plate 25 · Page 386

Traddles Makes a Figure in Parliament and I Report Him

[P L A T E   A]

a) The signature looks like "PWZ" with a short tail from the *Z* below it.
b) The picture frame below Demosthenes is unshaded except for a bit at the right.
c) The lower part of the parrot cage is not well defined.
d) The end of a pencil is in David's mouth.
e) The book marked *Reports* on the pile behind David is shaded on top by lines parallel to the spine.

[P L A T E   B]

a) There is no signature.
b) The left side and top of the picture frame below Demosthenes are shaded.
c) The lower part of the parrot cage is dark, with horizontal and vertical lines.
d) David's pencil extends beyond his mouth on both sides.
e) The book of *Reports* is shaded by lines parallel to the top and bottom edges and at right angles to the spine.

Traddles makes a figure in parliament, and I report him

Traddles makes a figure in parliament and I report him

Part XIII · Plate 26 · Page 413

The Wanderer

[P L A T E   A]

a) The signature ends in a wavy line at the left.
b) The framed picture to the right of the map of the world is clearly shown and stands out much lighter than the background.
c) The jug on the table which touches David's hands is shaded by vertical lines.
d) David's face is shaded by diagonal lines.
e) The banjo clock at the right is shaded by vertical lines.
f) The side of David's hat is shaded by horizontal lines in the lighter portions.
g) The top of the panel back of Peggotty and David is shown by three parallel lines.

[P L A T E   B]

a) The signature ends at the left in a line with several small loops.
b) The picture to the right of the map is darkened to match the background.
c) The jug in front of David is shaded by horizontal lines.
d) David's face is shaded by horizontal lines.
e) The banjo clock is shaded by crossed horizontal and vertical lines.
f) The side of David's hat is shaded by slightly curved vertical lines in the lighter portion.
g) The top of the panel is shown by two parallel lines. The whole of this plate was made much darker than the preceding by the addition of crisscross shade lines.

The Wanderer.

The Wanderer

Part XIV · Plate 27 · Page 420

Traddles and I in Conference with the Misses Spenlow

The text speaks of a clock on the mantel, but none is shown in the illustration.

[PLATE A]

a) The signature resembles "RIIZ," with a tail to the *Z* that has one loop but ends in a straight line to the left. There is a short vertical mark a short distance after the signature which may be a figure 1 or simply a scratch.

b) The picture at the left is marked *The Momentous Question* and suggests Leap Year! The picture at the right is marked *The Last Appeal*. The Arcadia picture shows no birds in the sky.

c) The lower book at the right, on top of the organ, is marked *Music*.

d) David's right leg is shaded all the way down.

[PLATE B]

a) The signature is similar to that in the preceding plate, but it ends at the left in a sharp downward angle.

b) The left and right pictures are not labeled. The Arcadia picture shows two birds in the sky.

c) The book at the right on the organ is unmarked.

d) David's right leg is half-white below the knee.

Traddles and I in conference with the Misses Spenlow.

Traddles and I in conference with the Misses Spenlow.

Part XIV · Plate 28 · Page 447

I Am Married

[P L A T E   A]

a) The signatures are very similar in both plates and look like "RIIZ." In Plate A the *Z* begins with a curve open to the left, and this, with the top line of the letter, resembles a figure 2. Following the diagonal line of the *Z* comes a curve in the form of the figure 3, which ends in a wiggly line to the left.
b) The panel above the beadle's staff is marked *Deborah Browne, Spinster*.
c) To the left and somewhat higher up, the head on the wall has either no beard or else Galways.
d) All four candlesticks on the pulpit are without extinguishers or candles.
e) The woman standing on the stairway is not shaded to any great extent.

[P L A T E   B]

a) The signature is similar to the preceding, but both the top and the bottom loops of the *Z* are closed curves.
b) The panel is marked *Deborah Patten, Spinster*.
c) The head on the wall has a pointed beard.
d) One of the candlesticks has an extinguisher on top.
e) The woman standing on the stairway has her arm and skirt shaded by vertical lines, with diagonals near the top.

I am Married.

I am Married.

Our Housekeeping

The two plates differ to an unusual extent. Neither is signed by the artist. Although the illustration shows confusion such as probably never was and more than Dickens himself described, it actually makes the appearance of the room more real.

[PLATE A]

a) At the extreme left of the top shelf, there are two books lying flat above the others.
b) The pickle jar has bulging sides.
c) The top of the bookcase is shown by one, two, and one parallel lines.
d) Just above David's left elbow there is a vertical book to the left of an inclined one.
e) Neither carving knife nor carving fork shows guards.
f) Traddles' right forefinger is almost touching a tumbler.
g) The basket (?) in front of the sewing box on the floor shows a small loop within the loop of the drawstring.
h) The corkscrew at Traddles' foot points to the lower left.
ı) Below the doghouse at the left there is a thick book and a thin one.

[PLATE B]

a) There is only one book lying flat at the left end of the top shelf.
b) The pickle jar has straight parallel sides.
c) The top line of the bookcase shows one, three, and two(?) lines.
d) There is no vertical book above David's elbow.
e) Both knife and fork show guards.
f) There is no tumbler near Traddles' forefinger.
g) The drawstring of the basket(?) in front of the sewing box on the floor forms only a simple loop.
h) The corkscrew at Traddles' foot points to the right.
ı) Below the doghouse there are two thick books.

Our Housekeeping.

Our Housekeeping.

Mr. Dick Fulfils My Aunt's Prediction

[P L A T E A]

a) The signature looks like "RIIZ," the last letter beginning with a straight line and ending in a small loop followed by a slightly curved line and a few wiggles.

b) The book leaning against the wastepaper basket is shaded by lines parallel to the spine.

c) There is no paper on the floor to the left of the envelope near the wastepaper basket.

d) Mrs. Markleham's newspaper shows no division into columns.

e) All the books on the top shelf of the bookcase stand erect.

f) The book in Dr. Strong's hand and the one standing in an inclined position before him show lines at right angles to the binding edge, representing printing.

[P L A T E B]

a) The tail of the *Z* forms a loop which cuts into the *H*, then extends to the left in a long wiggly line.

b) The book against the wastepaper basket is shaded by lines at right angles to the spine.

c) There is a piece of paper on the floor below Mrs. Strong's knee.

d) Mrs. Markleham's newspaper shows divisions at the top into three columns.

e) Three of the books on the top shelf lean slightly to the left.

f) The pages of Dr. Strong's two books are blank except for a few shade lines.

Mr Dick fulfils my Aunt's prediction.

Mr. Dick fulfils my Aunt's prediction

The River

This is the first and only "dark plate" in *David Copperfield* and the second etched by "Phiz," the first being Plate 35 of *Dombey and Son*. Duplicate plates were etched, neither signed. The differences between them are hard to describe but easily seen. Both show machine ruling.

[P L A T E   A]

a) The machine ruling that is most prominent and best seen is in the water in the left portion of the plate, where it is horizontal. There is also diagonal machine ruling sloping downward toward the left in the clouds and in the right upper part of the plate. The clouds are shown by lighter patches burnished in but not by etched freehand lines.

b) David's cravat is clearly shown, and the collar of his waistcoat is quite light.

c) The horizontal wooden brace upon which Peggotty's hand rests ends at the left without a sharp point.

d) Three of the chimneys in the far distance are smoking. To the right of the bridge and to the right of the two towers, vertical shade lines seem to represent foliage.

[P L A T E   B]

a) The machine ruling is diagonal, sloping downward from right to left. The clouds are shown by freehand etching of more or less horizontal lines, the unevenness showing the handwork. In the sky at the left there are curved black lines representing the edges of the clouds.

b) David's cravat is not clearly shown, and his waistcoat is uniformly dark.

c) The wooden brace upon which Peggotty's hand rests ends at the left upper edge in a point.

d) Two chimneys are smoking. To the right of the two towers there is another dome and several chimneys.

The River

The River.

Mr. Peggotty's Dream Comes True

[PLATE A]

a) The signature looks like "RIIZ," with the *Z* ending in a wiggly line extending far to the left.
b) The picture near David's face shows a fisherman wearing a sou'wester and with a child at his feet.
c) The watch on the wall at the left shows the time to be half-past two.
d) The window casing is not shaded.
e) The dodger on the floor near the bouquet is marked *Bal Masq.* . . .
f) The end of the sewing box (they do like to drop these and spill the contents) is shaded with many vertical and a few horizontal lines.
g) The upper card shows only a single pip in one corner. The rectangle near the leg of the chair is apparently a torn ace of hearts.
h) David's coat skirts do not end above the table top.

[PLATE B]

a) The signature ends in a curved line with a loop and extends as a broken line, then with wiggles, far to the left.
b) The fisherman in the picture is talking to a woman.
c) The watch shows only one hand pointing between twelve and one o'clock.
d) The window casing is shaded by vertical lines.
e) The dodger on the floor is marked *Theare.*
f) The end of the sewing box is shaded by horizontal and diagonal lines.
g) The upper card shows four pips, and the rectangle near the leg of the chair seems to be an ace.
h) David's coat skirts end above the line of the table top.

Mr Peggottys dream comes true

Mr. Peggotty's dream comes true.

Restoration of Mutual Confidence between Mr. and Mrs. Micawber

[P L A T E   A]

a) The signature ends in a straight line below the word *PHIZ*.
b) The jumping jack near the clock has his left elbow turned outward.
c) Between the pincushion and the ball of yarn spilled from the sewing basket there are two spools.
d) Below the plant in the window at the right there is only the barest suggestion of a flowerpot.
e) Mr. Dick's tie has no polka dots.
f) David's face is shaded by vertical lines except at the left, where there are short diagonals at his temple.
g) At the lower left the book on the floor is marked *Warbler*, and that on the chair *Comic Songs*.

[P L A T E   B]

a) The signature is entirely surrounded by an oval flourish.
b) The jumping jack has his left elbow turned inward.
c) Near the sewing basket the two objects between the pincushion and the ball of yarn are not recognizable as spools.
d) The plant at the window stands in a half-drawn, but recognizable, flowerpot.
e) Mr. Dick wears a polka-dot tie.
f) David's entire face except his right temple is shaded by slightly inclined lines.
g) The book on the floor in the lower left corner is marked *Psalmody*, and that on the chair *Glees*.

Restoration of mutual confidence between Mr. and Mrs. Micawber

Restoration of mutual confidence between Mr. and Mrs. Micawber

Part XVII · Plate 34 · Page 544

My Child-Wife's Old Companion

[PLATE A]

a) The signature is unusual: simply *P* and the first line of *H*, or *P* and *Z* in a combination that looks like the letter *R* in script, underlined and ending in a curve open to the left.

b) The guitar strings form a cross and are continuous single lines.

c) The clasp of the book on the floor is represented by a single line.

d) The ribbon hanging from Dora's bonnet is shaded.

e) The upper corner of David's chair is unshaded.

f) The push plates on the door are well defined.

g) There is a butterfly on the inkwell on the desk.

h) The front of the doghouse, below the entrance, is shaded by diagonal lines.

[PLATE B]

a) The signature is in the same position as in Plate A but is faint.

b) One of the two guitar strings, where it crosses the belly, is not continuous but is offset, and for a short distance the continuation is parallel with the broken end.

c) The clasp of the book on the floor shows two lines.

d) The ribbon hanging from Dora's bonnet is white.

e) The upper corner of David's chair is shaded.

f) The push plates on the door are poorly defined.

g) There is no butterfly on the inkwell.

h) The front of the doghouse is shaded by lines parallel to the base.

My child-wife's old companion

My child-wife's old companion

Part XVIII · Plate 35 · Page 566

I Am the Bearer of Evil Tidings

[PLATE A]

a) The plate is unsigned.
b) The rear end of the horse in the picture in the center is unshaded.
c) There is no button on the lid of the tobacco jar on the mantel.
d) Rosa Dartle's face is half-shaded.
e) The left point of David's collar shows beyond his chin.
f) There is no number on the plate.

[PLATE B]

a) The signature at the lower right consists of the letter *P*, a straight line, and an encircling curve.
b) The rear end of the horse is shaded by vertical lines.
c) There is a button on the lid of the tobacco jar.
d) Rosa Dartle's face is unshaded.
e) The left point of David's collar does not show near his chin.
f) At the lower left there is a very small *2*, crossed out by a line sloping downward from right to left. It does not show in the reproduction.

I am the bearer of evil tidings

I am the bearer of evil tidings

Part XVIII · Plate 36 · Page 575

The Emigrants

[P L A T E   A]

a) The plate is unsigned.

b) The square window at the upper right, touched by the child's hand, is defined at the top and bottom by single lines only.

c) Two nails show in the label on the chest in the lower left center.

d) The cloth under the woman in the lower left corner does not hang down into the margin of the picture.

e) The lantern at the top center shows a white square where the vertical and horizontal bars cross.

f) There are no lines crossing the shade lines in the ceiling above the Irishman with the glass at the upper right.

[P L A T E   B]

a) This plate is signed *PZ* on the side of the chest in the lower left.

b) The square window is defined by three lines above and two below.

c) The label on the chest shows four nailheads.

d) The cloth at the lower left hangs down, unshaded, in the margin.

e) The lantern at the top shows three parallel horizontal lines and three vertical ones crossing at the center. The lines are broken where they cross, but there is no clearly marked white square.

f) The ceiling in the upper right has several lines crossing the shade lines.

The Emigrants.

Part XIX · Plate 37 · Page 605

I Am Shewn Two Interesting Penitents

[P L A T E   A]

a) The signature is *PZ*. There is a small loop beneath it and a tail extending to the left.
b) There is only one bar showing through the cell door above Uriah's head, and the casing above is shaded by horizontal lines.
c) At the upper left a third cell door shows three small dots in the place of rivets.
d) The left hand of the second man from the left is shaded by vertical lines.
e) The hinge edge of the door to Mr. Littimer's cell is shown by two parallel lines above the head of one of the guards.

[P L A T E   B]

a) The signature looks like "RIIZ." It has two loops in the tail.
b) There are two bars showing above Uriah's head.
c) The third cell door has three rivets near the top.
d) There is no shading on the left hand of the second man.
e) The hinge edge of Mr. Littimer's cell door is shown as a single line.

I am born for better events

Plate 37 A COPPERFIELD / 389

I am shewn two interesting penitents

Part XIX · Plate 38 · Page 615

A Stranger Calls To See Me

[P L A T E   A]

a) The plate is unsigned.
b) The face of Dora in the portrait is shaded by diagonal lines.
c) In the picture of Peggotty's boathouse, there are either two persons in the foreground or one person and a post.
d) The doll on the chair wears shoes with straps around the ankles.
e) The tie on Mr. Peggotty's stock is dark.
f) The open book at Agnes' feet shows both pages with lines representing printing.

[P L A T E   B]

a) The signature *PHIZ* ends at the left in a line with loops.
b) The face of Dora in the portrait is shaded by vertical lines.
c) Peggotty's boathouse shows two figures sitting close together.
d) The doll on the chair wears no shoes.
e) The tie on Mr. Peggotty's stock is moderately light.
f) The open book on the floor beside Agnes shows one page with a picture.

A Stranger calls to see me

A Stranger calls to see me.

Part XX · Plate 39 · Frontispiece

Miss Betsy Pressing Her Nose against the Window

In an etching with foliage, it is possible to imagine all kinds of things among the leaves, probably not intended by the artist to represent anything. Thus, in Plate A, immediately back of Miss Betsy's right foot is a very small *2*, while in Plate B, somewhat farther back from her foot, appear the letters *Pell* . . . or *Pesl* . . . , where the *s* is the old-fashioned long *s*. Below it is the figure *2*.

See page 3.

[PLATE A]

a) The signatures to both plates are very small and plain. Plate A gives the artist's name as *RIIZ*.
b) The gate shows three pickets.
c) Four or five gravestones show through the trees.
d). The shading on the ball at the upper corner of the house is by vertical lines.
e) The square tablet over the bay window shows the letter *C*.
f) Miss Betsy's purse is attached to her wrist by three strings. There is no bracelet on her wrist.
g) One of the sticks back of the barrel leans against the house, with its tip resting higher than the top of the window.
h) The bird on the ground is holding its tail almost horizontally.

[PLATE B]

a) The signature looks like "PIIIZ" with no crossbar to the *H*.
b) The gate has two pickets.
c) Two gravestones show through the trees.
d) The shading of the ball is by lines which more or less follow its outline.
e) The tablet shows no large letter.
f) Miss Betsy's purse has one single cord, then two close together, which are attached to a bracelet on her wrist.
g) The sticks leaning against the window do not reach above it.
h) The bird's tail points upward at an angle of 45°.

See page 3.

Part XX · Plate 40 · Etched Title

Peggotty's House

Hablôt K. Browne, throughout *David Copperfield*, made the mistake of showing Peggotty's house as an overturned boat, although Dickens distinctly indicates that it was right side up. For the purpose of an interesting illustration, Browne's way, of course, was the better, even though it did not follow the text.

The publishers' imprint, London/Bradbury & Evans, Bouverie Street/1850, is below the etched vignette of Peggotty's house.

[PLATE A]

a) The signature is small; the final *Z* begins with a straight line and ends at the bottom with a curve of one loop. The *H* has no crossbar.

b) The window near the barrel shows white at the left. Three boards repair the boat just above the clothesline, upon which there are four stockings (?).

c) The boat hook leaning against the house at the right has both a hook and a spike at the end.

[PLATE B]

a) The final *Z* of the signature has a curve above it. There is a dot over the *I*, and the *H* has a crossbar. The tail of the *Z* extends under the signature with a small loop, but otherwise it is straight.

b) The window shows a shaded casing. Two boards repair the boat above the clothesline, which has five objects hanging from it.

c) The boat hook has only a hook at the end.

BLEAK HOUSE

Sixteen months after the completion of *David Copperfield*, *Bleak House* was begun. It appeared, as usual, in twenty monthly parts, the nineteenth and twentieth together, but it differed from preceding novels in having blue wrappers instead of green. In general appearance, however, it was similar to those that had gone before and likewise had a border design by Hablôt K. Browne on the front. The first number was put on sale in March, 1852, and the last in September, 1853. Each part contained 2 etchings by Browne, only 10 of which were made in duplicate, so that the entire number of steels for the book was 50. The 10 that were duplicated were all so-called "dark plates," which apparently were all printed directly from the steels, while the remaining 30 plates were both lithographed and printed from the steels, and these impressions were mixed indiscriminately when placed in the monthly parts. These lithographs, of course, were exactly the same as the prints from the steels, but they can usually be distinguished by a muddier appearance. Only 2 dark plates had been issued previously, No. 35 of *Dombey and Son* and No. 31 of *David Copperfield*. After the 10 in *Bleak House*, there were 8 etched for *Little Dorrit*. The 10 dark plates in *Bleak House* which were etched in duplicate are Plates 24, 26, 28, 29, 32, 34, 35, 36, 38, and the Frontispiece.

The duplicate plates were not numbered, but Hatton and Cleaver say that the first plates may usually be distinguished by a somewhat flat appearance, while the second plates, having probably received more work, "were strengthened in the chiaroscuro."

In the following pages, only the 10 duplicated plates are described. There are many small differences, many trivial, but only the more easily seen are listed here.

Between the dates of appearance of the final part of *David Copperfield* and the beginning of *Bleak House* in March, 1852, very few published works illustrated by Browne appeared; but, since so many books illustrated by him came out the next year and a half while *Bleak House* was being issued—that is, between March, 1852, and September, 1853—it is probable that some had been etched in the intervening period. Besides the 50 etchings for Dickens, in those nineteen months, "Phiz" made 46 etchings for Lever's *The Daltons*, 42 for Smedley's *Lewis Arundel*, and 18 for Ainsworth's *Crichton* and 16 for his *Revelations of London*. There were also a few minor etchings.

Part XII · Plate 24 · Page 361

The Ghost's Walk

This is the first of the *Bleak House* dark plates and is the first plate in the book to be etched in duplicate. Neither plate is signed by the artist.

[P L A T E   A]

a) The checkered spots in the windows at the left are staggered, that is, they appear to lie in diagonal lines.
b) The edge of the shield and the paws of the griffin are white.
c) There is a distinct black vertical line near the left margin forming the boundary of the panel on the stairway.
d) The lower right corner shows markings on the ground resembling "2 = D."
e) The dots in the sky are staggered.

[P L A T E   B]

a) The light dots in the windows at the left lie in straight vertical lines.
b) The edge of the shield and the paws of the griffin are shaded.
c) There is no distinct line marking the left limit of the stairway.
d) There are many lines of horizontal dots in the lower right corner.
e) The light dots in the sky lie in vertical and horizontal lines.

The Ghost's Walk.

Part XIII · Plate 26 · Page 397

Sunset in the Long Drawing-Room at Chesney Wold

This is the second of the *Bleak House* dark plates.

[P L A T E   A]

a) The sheet music below the finger board of the guitar is marked with parallel lines to represent staves.
b) Just above the fringes of the scarf lying on the chair back at the right there are two parallel lines, and a third is just above these two.
c) There is no black dot in the center of the book or paper lying on the table at the far right.
d) The panel just back of the jewel box on the same table shows a sketch somewhat resembling a cat with one paw showing below the head.

[P L A T E   B]

a) The sheet music below the guitar seems to have printing and not music staves on the front.
b) There are no prominent lines parallel to the line of the fringes of the scarf, but, instead, there are two rows of short, parallel, vertical lines.
c) There is a black dot in the center of the paper on the table.
d) The panel back of the jewel box shows two figures close together and within an irregular circular border.

Sunset in the long Drawing-room at Chesney Wold.

Part XIV · Plate 28 · Page 442

Tom All Alone's

This is the third dark plate for *Bleak House*.

[P L A T E A]

a) At the bottom of the right pilaster supporting the roof over the door at the lower left there is a dark oval.
b) The window in the tower in the background clearly shows a circular rose window and two long windows below.

[P L A T E B]

a) There is no ornament in the base of the pilaster.
b) The church window is very sketchy.

Tom all alone's.

A New Meaning in the Roman

This, the fourth dark plate, shows more differences between the original and the duplicate than any of those preceding. It is not signed by the artist.

[PLATE A]

a) Between the two rugs in the lower right corner there are two lines separating the boards of the floor.

b) The left candle stub on the table is dark, the right one light.

c) The picture hanging in the shield-shaped decoration at the left of the center cabinet shows a very sketchy frame and no picture cord. There is no design in the oval above it, and there are two festoons still higher up.

d) Below the cornice and above the bookcase at the extreme right there are decorative black lines.

e) The lower of the two ribbons floating from the Roman's laurel wreath almost touches his cloak.

f) There are two amoretti back of the Roman.

[PLATE B]

a) Between the two rugs there is only a single joint separating two floor boards.

b) The left candle stub is white, the right one is dark.

c) The picture within the shield has a fairly well-outlined frame, and there is a single cord suspending it. There is a design in the oval above it, and the festoon is in one long curve.

d) The wall between the cornice and the bookcase at the right shows no decoration and is simply shaded with vertical lines.

e) The ribbon from the Roman's wreath does not come near his cloak.

f) There is only one amoretto back of the Roman.

Part XVI · Plate 32 · Page 512

Shadow

This is the fifth dark plate etched for *Bleak House.*

[PLATE A]

a) The *Murder* poster shows the upper left corner turned down. The pound sign has a crossbar.
b) Below the poster there are one, two, and one lines to represent the upper part of the wainscot.
c) The decorations on the vase in the archway extend entirely across it.

[PLATE B]

a) The poster has no turned-down corner, and the pound sign has no crossbar.
b) Below the poster, the upper lines of the wainscot are one and two only; the fourth is missing.
c) The decorations on the vase are very sketchy and cover only a small part of it.

Part XVII · Plate 34 · Page 544

The Lonely Figure

This is the sixth of the dark plates.

[P L A T E   A]

a) The horsecollar, as well as the beam to which it is attached, is drawn partly as a heavy single line and partly as two lines so close together that they seem like one. Near the collar the beam is definitely a single line.

b) At the left there are three brick kilns.

c) In general, this plate is lighter in color than its duplicate, but in the lower right it is somewhat darker.

[P L A T E   B]

a) The collar and the beam to which it is attached are double lines.

b) At the left there are only two brick kilns.

c) The lower right corner of the plate is lighter than Plate A, and the bricks and straw are rather sketchily drawn there.

Part XVIII · Plate 36 · Page 547

The Night

This is the seventh *Bleak House* dark plate. It is neither signed nor numbered.

[P L A T E A]

a) The flame in the lamp in the center is nearly white. Below the lamp housing at the top of the post there are two projections to the left.
b) At the lower left the tripod-like structure, which looks like the mast of a sunken vessel, has at least six or seven lines extending to the water.

$\big[$ P L A T E B $\big]$

a) The flame in the street lamp in the center is dim. There is only one bar
projecting to the left from the lampost.

b) At the lower left there are only four dark lines extending from the mast to
the water.

Part XVIII · Plate 37 · Page 576

The Morning

This is the eighth of the dark plates. Said one writer: "This is one of the best plates Hablôt K. Browne ever did." I most emphatically disagree.

[P L A T E   A]

a) Only the flame shows in the lantern hanging from the arch.
b) Three bars are reflected in the water at the lower left. They are poorly defined and blurred and do not extend upward to the steps.

[P L A T E   B]

a) The stub of a candle, the wick, and the flame are shown in the lantern.
b) Three bars are reflected below the steps, each drawn with two lines and all extending nearly to the lowest step.

The Mausoleum at Chesney Wold

This is the ninth dark plate. Like all the others in *Bleak House*, it is a gloomy picture and reflects the dreary tone of the story itself. "Phiz" was much more in his element in the humorous atmosphere of the light plates. Neither plate is signed by the artist.

[P L A T E   A]

a) There are many differences in the drawing of the trees and the ferns in the foreground, but they are impossible to describe in words. The quickest test of this plate is the length of the horizontal lines of the pool of water at the bottom of the plate. In Plate A they extend to within 5 mm. of the left frame of the etching.

b) The lines bounding the etching on three sides are fairly heavy at the left and top and meet at the upper right corner with a fainter vertical line. There are no distinct dots marking the lower ends of the vertical lines.

c) The lines of dots shading the lower left corner are approximately horizontal.

[P L A T E   B]

a) The lines of the pool end at approximately 16 mm. from the left frame.

b) The frame lines are thin and show a slight break at the upper right corner. Each vertical line has a small black dot at the lower end.

c) The lines of dots shading the lower left corner slant downward from left to right.

Parts XIX and XX · Frontispiece

This is the tenth and last of the dark plates and also the tenth and last etched in duplicate. There are many differences in shading and in the forms of the branches of the trees, but they are impossible to describe in words.

[PLATE A]

a) The lower window of the right-hand tower is sketchy and does not show divisions into panes.
b) Beginning at the left just to the right of the trees, the sky line of roofs shows, first, a chimney with three parts; second, a dome; third, a chimney in three parts, the central one extending higher than the dome and almost as high as the staff above it; and, fourth, a cluster of chimney pots whose central one is almost as tall as the preceding cluster.
c) The short building at the right end of the cluster of buildings shows a window which forms about three-fourths of a circle above the foliage.

[PLATE B]

a) The lower window mullions have a distinct cross between the panes.
b) The first chimney shows only two parts, the second a dome, the third a three-part chimney reaching no higher than the dome, and the fourth a cluster of chimney pots, all narrow and consisting of a single one shorter than the preceding groups and three still shorter.
c) The window in the far building at the right shows only a very small part of the circular window.

FRONTISPIECE.

LITTLE DORRIT

Bleak House was finished in September, 1853, and fifteen months later, in December, 1855, *Little Dorrit* was begun. Like its predecessors, it appeared in twenty monthly parts, the final numbers, 19 and 20, together as one in June, 1857. Like *Bleak House*, this novel had blue wrappers. Apparently, "Phiz" found that horizontal plates allowed him greater freedom, for in this book the majority of the plates were so etched. Of the 40 plates, 27 are horizontal and 13 vertical. Only 9 plates were etched in duplicate, 7 of them dark plates and 2 of the usual kind, making a total of 49 steels for the book. The 2 ordinary plates that were duplicated were No. 21, "The Travellers," and No. 22, "The Family Dignity Is Affronted," both of them appearing in Part XI. One dark plate was issued with each of the first five parts, none with Part VI, and one each with Parts VII and VIII. An eighth dark plate, No. 37, "Damocles," appeared in Part XIX, page 595, but it was not duplicated. Hatton and Cleaver (p. 307) said that all the dark plates were horizontal, but this is incorrect, for "Little Dorrit's Party" and "Damocles" are vertical.

Hatton and Cleaver also say that Plate 17, Part IX, page 257, shows distinct signs of machine ruling, although they did not include it among the dark plates. I cannot agree with this, for the nearly parallel background lines of this plate are not machine-ruled but etched freehand. They are not perfectly straight and are not continuous but broken. But this plate is not alone among the light plates in having freehand ruling, for Plate 19, page 290, for example, shows the same thing. There is, however, an earlier plate in *Dombey and Son*, No. 20, page 316, which shows lines in two directions that appear actually to have been done mechanically.

There is another series of straight lines which should be mentioned here, namely, rouletted dots in many plates, most of them clearly made with the wheel, either single or double, held loosely in the hand without a guiding straightedge. These dots were not used on any of the *Pickwick* plates but were first used on Plate 1 of *Nicholas Nickleby* and later, with a few exceptions, on all those that followed—but not always to their great improvement. The lines of dots are usually quite irregularly spaced, for example, in Plate 5, page 73, and Plate 33, page 519, of *Little Dorrit*, or even in waves, as in Plate 26, page 410. In rare cases the lines run in straight lines to form a pattern like rows of corn in a cornfield, as though the roulette wheel were held against a straightedge, e.g., Plate 9, page 134, in part. However, since none of these plates was duplicated, they do not belong in this book but are mentioned only for the record.

Apparently, the dark plates were not entirely satisfactory, for, with the exception of "Damocles" on page 595, they ended with Plate 16, in Part VIII, on page 250, and none was used thereafter. None of the plates, either dark or light, in *Little Dorrit* was signed by the artist, and, since practically all are much more sketchy and scratchy than Browne's usual drawings and seem to show haste or carelessness, this is not surprising.

After the conclusion of *Bleak House*, in September, 1853, and before the beginning of *Little Dorrit*, in December, 1855, "Phiz" etched 40 plates for Lever's *Dodd Family Abroad*, 20 for Smith's *Pottleton Legacy*, and 29 for Smedley's *Harry Coverdale's Courtship*. He also drew designs for at least 42 woodcuts. During the issue of *Little Dorrit*, December, 1855, to June, 1857, there were 49 etchings for that work, 40 for Lever's *Martins of Cro' Martin*, 13 for Mrs. Stowe's *Minister's Wooing*, a small number of plates for reissues of Fielding and Smollett, and a considerable number of woodcuts for *Nuts and Nutcrackers*.

Following *Little Dorrit* came *A Tale of Two Cities* in 1859 with 16 plates by Browne, but none of them was duplicated. This ended the tieup between him and Dickens, and the following novels were illustrated by different artists: *Our Mutual Friend*, 1864–65, by Marcus Stone, and *The Mystery of Edwin Drood*, 1870, by S. Luke Fildes. Since *Little Dorrit* contained the last of the duplicated plates, it is the last of the books considered here.

Chapman and Hall were Dickens' publishers from the beginning of *Pickwick*, in 1836, to the ending of *Martin Chuzzlewit* in 1843. He then changed to Bradbury and Evans, who had been printing the books, with the beginning of *Dombey and Son*, in 1846, and continued with them until the ending of *Little Dorrit* in 1857. For all his subsequent books he returned to his original publishers.

Part I · Plate 1 · Page 2

The Birds in the Cage

Etched in duplicate. Neither one is signed. In both, the machine ruling in the spandrels is horizontal only.

[PLATE A]

a) The machine ruling is entirely horizontal, best seen in the lower left corner or in the lighter portions of the plate, such as the window or the sun-lighted column.
b) The draughts board is clearly shown, six squares in the center are complete, and the central horizontal line extends to the line at the left.
c) The links in the chain at the right are so drawn that alternate ones are almost exactly edgewise.

[PLATE B]

a) The machine ruling in the spandrels is horizontal only, but in the remainder of the plate it is both horizontal and diagonal, the latter sloping downward from left to right. This can be seen in the light from the window, in the light on the wall at the right, and clearly in the extreme lower left corner, where there is a small triangle of light. Lines apparently sloping downward from right to left are optical illusions.
b) The draughts board is poorly drawn: only two of the central squares are complete, and the horizontal line at the center does not reach the left line.
c) The links of the chain are hanging in such a position that alternate links show opposite sides equally.

The Birds in the Cage.

The Room with the Portrait

This is the second of the duplicated plates and the second of the dark plates in the book. Both are machine-ruled horizontally and diagonally downward to the left.

[P L A T E   A]

a) Lying on the trunk in the lower left part of the picture are several sheets of paper only slightly bent.
b) The largest of the books lying against this trunk has two labels on the spine.
c) The sheet of paper at the left of the inkwell projects slightly over the edge toward the chair.
d) At the right of the inkwell there are some flat sheets and a roll of paper.
e) The chest on the table shows metal corners and a lock.
f) On top of the chest a sheaf of papers rests on a roll, and at the right of this a small piece of paper projects over the edge.
g) The clock seen through the doorway points to five minutes of three.

[P L A T E   B]

a) The article lying on the trunk is either a piece of cloth or a much-crumpled sheet of paper.
b) The large book has a single label on the spine.
c) The sheet of paper at the left of the inkwell lies entirely on the table and does not project over the edge.
d) There is no roll of paper on the desk at the right of the inkwell.
e) The chest on the table shows neither lock nor corners.
f) There is no paper to the right of the bundle on the chest, but there is a fairly large sheet at the left which hangs down over the side.
g) The clock seen through the doorway shows the time is four o'clock.

Making Off

This is the third plate etched in duplicate, the third dark plate, and one of the three better ones. The dreary landscape is so effectively shown that it makes one shudder to look at it.

[P L A T E A]

a) No falling leaves show against the sky below the branches extending to the left from the last tree at the right.
b) The tallest building at the horizon above the running man has a pointed top.
c) The root extending toward the bottom of the plate from the large tree in the foreground, and beginning just to the right of the hollow place in the trunk, has a round spot at the lower end which gives the root the appearance of the head of a dying ichthyosaurus.
d) There is a small tree on either side of the large one, almost touching the trunk in the drawing.

[P L A T E B]

a) Showing against the sky between the last two trees at the right there are five or six falling leaves.
b) At the horizon below these leaves, the tallest building has a square top.
c) The root extending toward the bottom of the plate resembles nothing in particular.
d) The two trees nearest the large central tree are more than their own diameters from the trunk.

Making off

Making off

Part IV · Plate 8 · Page 128

Little Dorrit's Party

This is the fourth dark plate and the fourth plate duplicated.

[P L A T E   A]

a) Maggy's left hand shows all her fingers.
b) The bow of Little Dorrit's bonnet hangs nearly straight down.
c) The second post of the fence leading around the barricade touches the fourth one, that is, the one at the back.
d) The arrow on the weather vane is not clearly defined.
e) The stars about the spire of the church are those of Ursa Major, with the steeple cutting through the center of the Dipper.
f) There is no lamppost showing at the corner where the fence swings around the church very near the right margin of the plate.
g) At the right center, the middle one of the three buildings in the distance shows a flat top, above which projects a group of chimney pots(?).
h) In the upper left, two tall chimney pots are separated by a short one.

[P L A T E   B]

a) Maggy's left hand shows only three fingers and the thumb.
b) The bow of Little Dorrit's bonnet slants to the right.
c) The second post around the barricade is farther to the left than in Plate A, so that it is within the line of the poles. The fourth post is some distance to the right.
d) The arrow of the weather vane is clearly shown.
e) The lower left star of the bowl of the Dipper is missing, but there are at least four additional stars, three of them between the weather vane and the margin at the top.
f) There is a lamppost where the fence turns around the church.
g) The middle house at the right has a pointed cornice with chimneys showing above.
h) Of the three chimney pots in the upper left corner, the middle one is the tallest.

The Ferry

While this is classed among the dark plates, actually it is not dark but sparkling with light. These plates might better have been called "machine-ruled." The ruling in this case is just as effective as in those with dark backgrounds, making "The Ferry" one of the best three in this group. In this plate the ruling is both horizontal and diagonal, clearly seen near the dog in the foreground. The diagonal lines appear to have been engraved, or at least burnished down, after the plate was etched. This is the fifth of the duplicated plates in *Little Dorrit*.

[PLATE A]

a) Disregarding the machine ruling, only a bit of the coat near the right arm of the man near the signpost is shaded.
b) The sign has just a few meaningless lines drawn upon it.
c) The sailboat is unshaded except by the machine engraving.
d) There are fifteen or sixteen birds in the sky.
e) The man in the rowboat is shaded by horizontal, machine-ruled lines as well as by a few dark curved lines.
f) At least two of the posts near the house at the left center are to the right of the left limit of the house; the third post is just at the end of the house.
g) The clump of trees at the left is shaded only by the machine engraving.

[PLATE B]

a) Besides the machine engraving, the man near the signboard has his coat shaded by dark vertical lines.
b) The sign has markings resembling letters.
c) The sailboat is partly shaded by vertical lines.
d) There are eleven birds in the sky.
e) The man in the rowboat is shaded by dark vertical lines.
f) The three posts near the left center are all beyond the left lines of the house.
g) The shadows in the trees at the left are indicated by vertical shading.

The Ferry

The Ferry

Visitors at the Works

This is the sixth of the dark plates. The machine ruling is in horizontal and diagonal lines.

[P L A T E   A]

a) The inside of Mr. F's aunt's bonnet is shaded by diagonal etched lines.

b) The drawstring of Mr. F's aunt's handbag forms a loop and then ends in a tassel, which lies below and clear of the bag itself.

c) The lower line of the molding which forms the top of the wainscoting above Mr. F's aunt's head is formed by two lines for over half the distance, the left portion showing two extra, but not parallel, lines. The upper line of the molding is formed by two lines farther apart.

d) The sprocket wheel at the lower right shows seven good teeth and a rudimentary one.

e) The smooth wheel adjacent to the sprocket wheel has four spokes.

f) The bend in the crankshaft at the right of the man's leg in the top center is at the left end.

g) The end of the vertical rod of the safety valve at the right center is curved.

[P L A T E   B]

a) The shading inside Mr. F's aunt's bonnet is vertical.

b) The loop of the drawstring of Mr. F's aunt's handbag is shown, but the end with the tassel is confused with the bag itself.

c) The molding of the wainscoting is formed by a double line between two single lines.

d) The sprocket wheel has nine teeth.

e) The smooth wheel near the sprocket wheel shows two spokes and part of a third.

f) The crankshaft at the top shows the bent portion in the middle.

g) The rod near the safety valve is vertical near the top.

Visitors at the Works.

Visitors at the Works

Part VIII · Plate 16 · Page 250

Floating Away

This is the seventh and last of the dark plates to be etched in duplicate. It has a machine-engraved background of horizontal lines, and, while there are a few diagonal lines in the sky, they appear to be hand-engraved.

[P L A T E   A]

a) The vertical shade lines on the back of Mr. Meagles' coat do not quite reach his collar, shoulder, or left arm.
b) The left edge of the moon does not quite touch the tree trunk.
c) The fence at the left shows five pickets.
d) On the bank just above the fence, the trees or tree-twins have the appearance of only two tree trunks.

[P L A T E   B]

a) The vertical shade lines on Mr. Meagles' coat reach collar, arm, and almost the shoulder.
b) The left edge of the moon is tangent to the tree.
c) The fence shows four pickets.
d) On the bank above the fence the trees have the appearance of three compound trunks.

Floating away.

Floating away.

Part XI · Plate 21 · Page 325

The Travellers

This is the first of the two ordinary, not dark, plates that were etched in duplicate. The etching is crude and unfinished and a very poor example of Browne's work, that is, if Browne himself actually made it and it was not the work of one of his assistants. The same may be said of many of the other etchings in *Little Dorrit*, as well as of some of *David Copperfield* and *Bleak House*. Undoubtedly the drawing was Browne's, though probably the actual etching was not.

[P L A T E   A]

a) The face of young Dorrit before the fireplace is shaded by diagonal lines. His shirt is shaded by similar lines, with only a few short, light lines crossing these near his tie and at the bottom. There is a black dot in the center of his monocle.
b) There are a few diagonal lines shading Mrs. General's right eye.
c) The lines of the leaded glass of the window at the upper right are strong and complete except at their ends.

[P L A T E   B]

a) Young Dorrit's face is not shaded. There are heavy lines crossing the diagonal shade lines of his shirt near his right arm. There is no dot in his monocle.
b) Mrs. General's eye is unshaded.
c) The crossed lines of the window are very sketchy, some formed by solid lines and some by dots.

The Travellers.

The Travellers.

The Family Dignity Is Affronted

This is the second and last of the two plates, not dark, that were etched in duplicate. Like the preceding, the drawing is unfinished in appearance, and, while Mr. Dorrit's figure is very good, the rest of the picture is rather mediocre.

[P L A T E   A]

a) The right trouser leg of the young man at the left shows two longitudinal stripes.
b) Young Dorrit's left trouser leg has a series of lines along the outside seam.
c) Mrs. Merdle's muff is shaded except for the upper left part.
d) The trunk on the man's shoulder at the right shows a handle at the end.
e) The traveling bags in the lower right corner are all quite heavily shaded, except the top of the one in the man's hands and the large bag on the ground.

[P L A T E   B]

a) The trouser leg of the man at the left has a single seam.
b) Young Dorrit's left trouser leg shows a single seam.
c) More than half of Mrs. Merdle's muff is unshaded.
d) The trunk on the shoulder of the man at the right shows a very rudimentary handle.
e) The traveling bags in the lower right corner are fairly light in color, parts of some being entirely white.

The family dignity is affronted.

The family dignity is affronted.